Street Atlas of
LEICESTER and DISTRICT

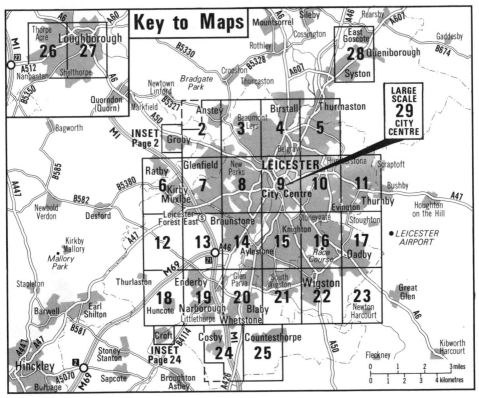

Key to Maps

LARGE SCALE **29** CITY CENTRE

EDITION 1

Reference

Motorway..................... ≡M1≡	House Numbers (Selected Roads)........ 2 45	Fire Station............... ■
	Railway..................... Station	Hospital.................., Ⓗ
Dual Carriageway...........	District Boundary............ –·–·–	Information Centre....... 𝒊
A Road....................... A6	Ambulance Station.......... ✚	Police Station............. ▲
B Road....................... B582	Car Parks (Selection)............. P	Post Office................. ●
One-Way Street (A roads only)...	Church or Chapel............ +	Toilet..................... ▽
Heavy Line on Drivers Left		

SCALE: 3½ inches to 1 mile

0	220yds.	¼	660yds.	½ mile
0	250m.	500m.	750 metres	

1:18,103

Copyright by the Publishers
Geographers' A-Z Map Company

Head Office: Vestry Road, Sevenoaks, Kent TN14 5EP Telephone Seve
Showrooms: 28 Gray's Inn Road, Holborn, London WC1X 8HX T

This Map is based upon the Ordnance Survey 1:10,560 & 1:10,000 Maps with the sanction of the C
Crown Copyright Reserved

D0273439

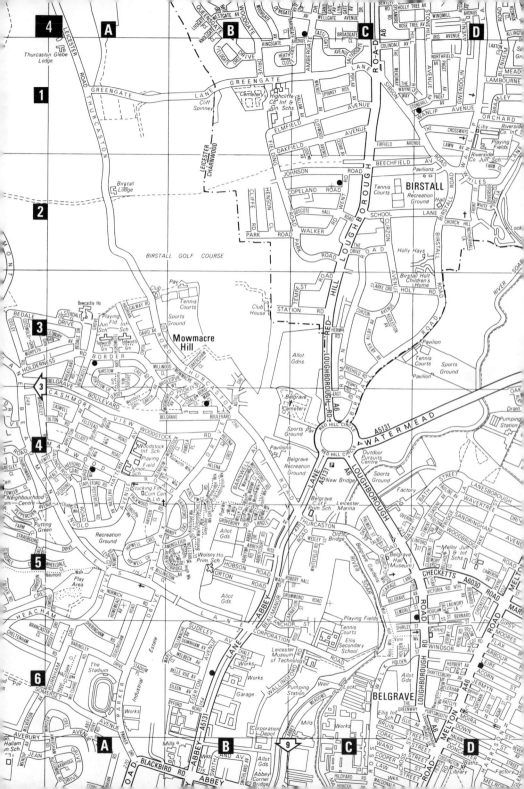

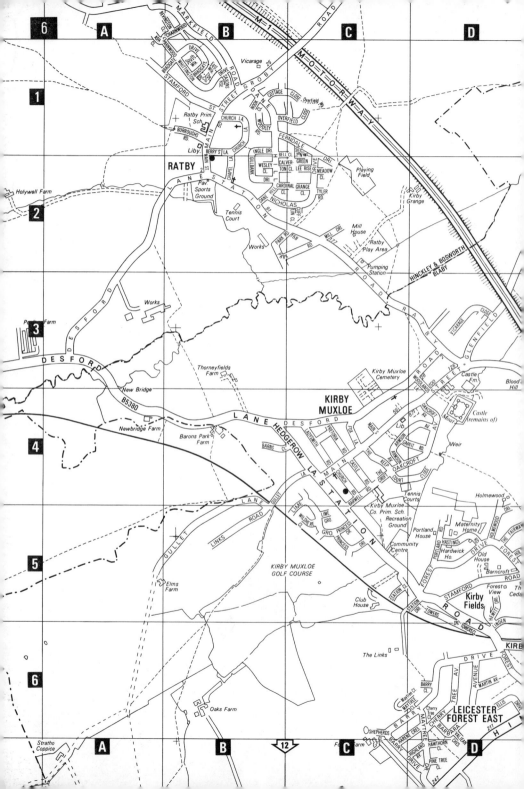

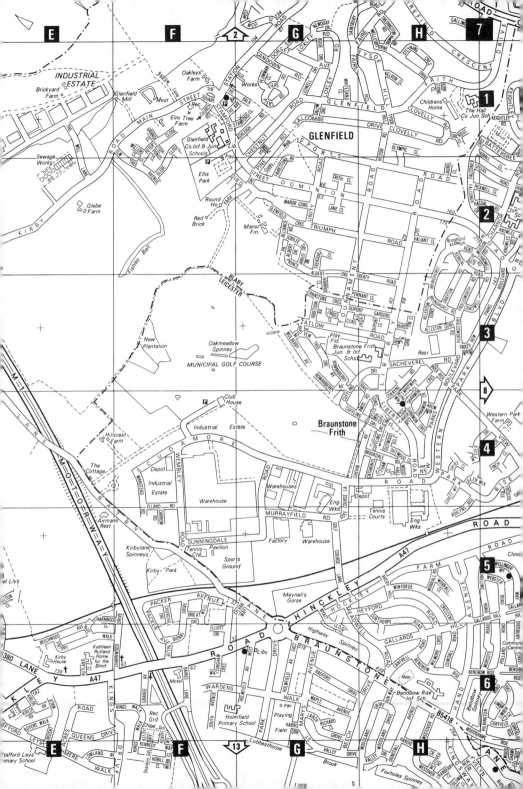

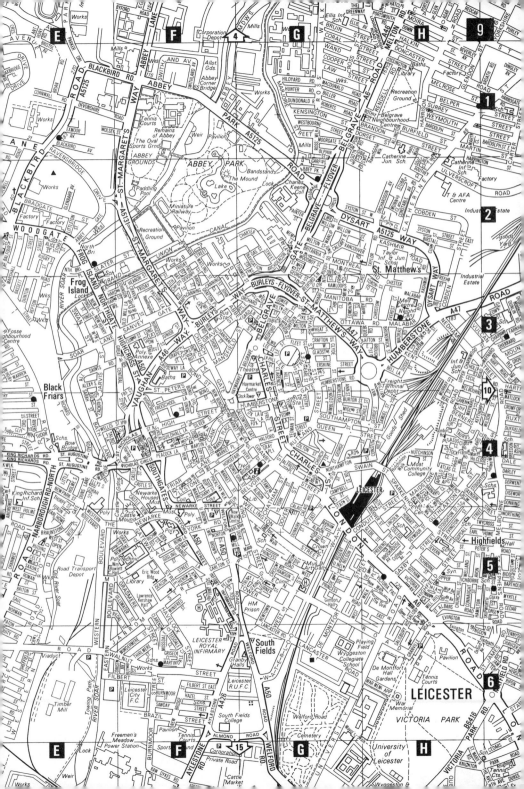

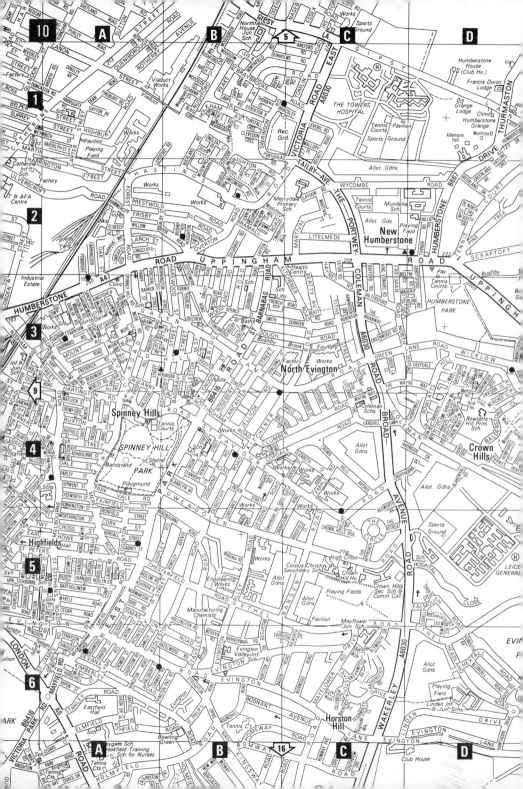

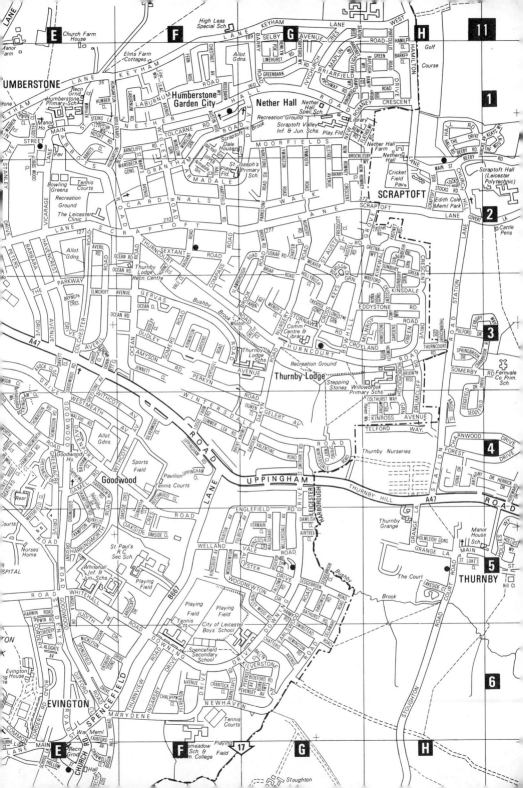

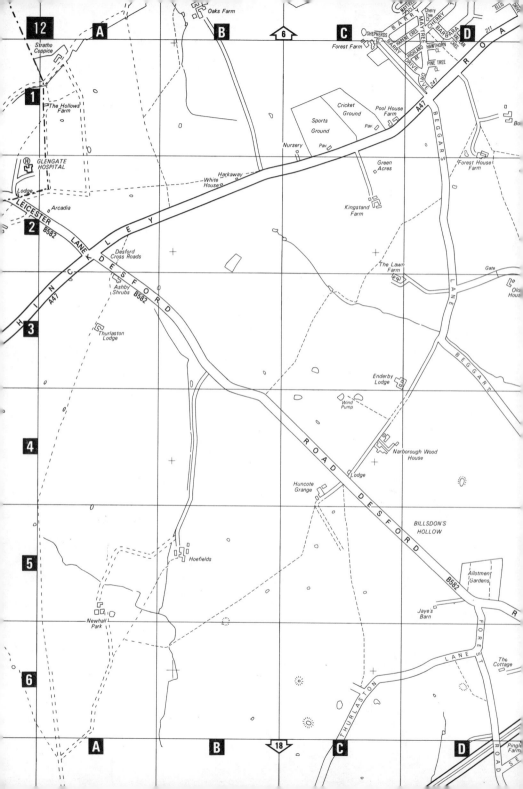

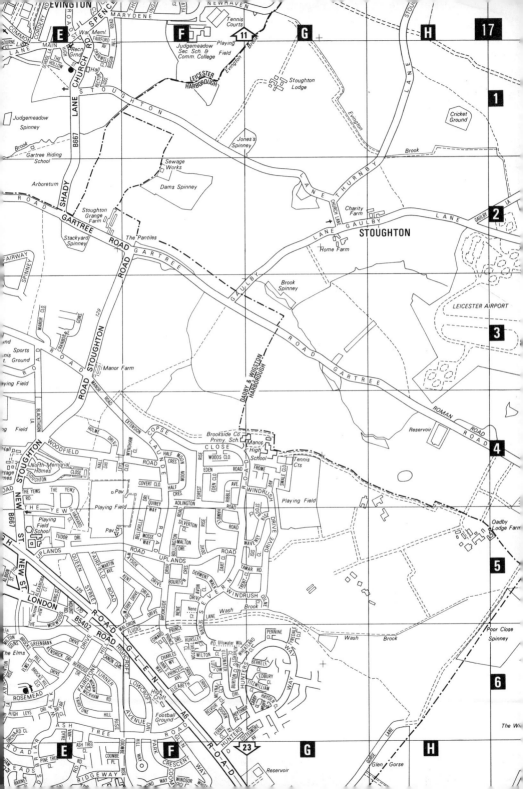

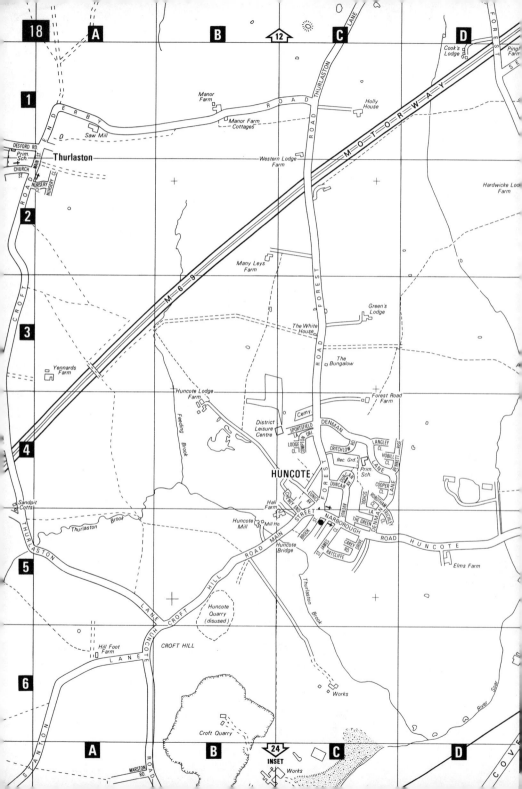

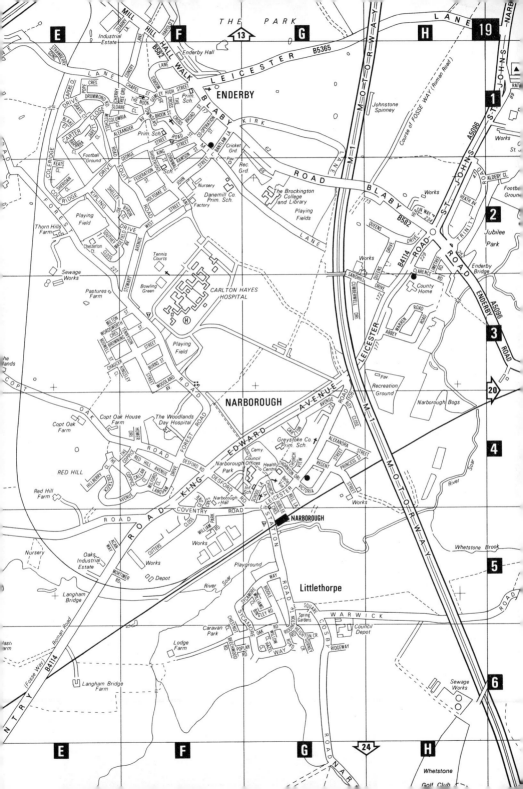

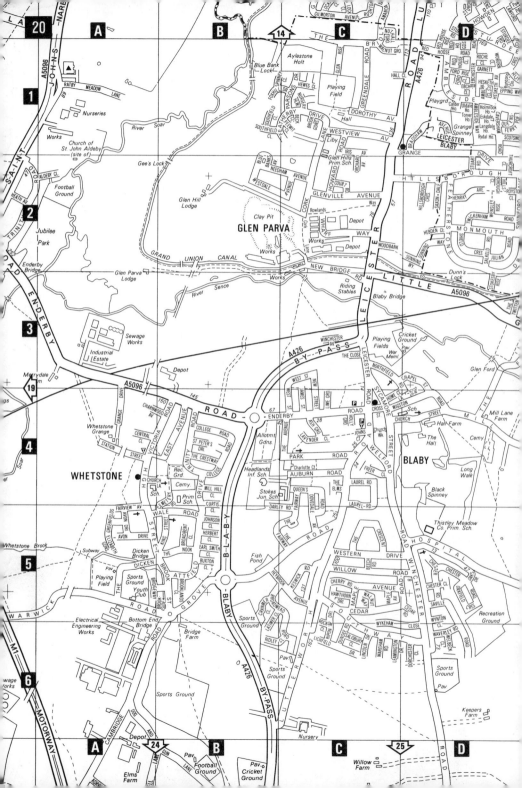

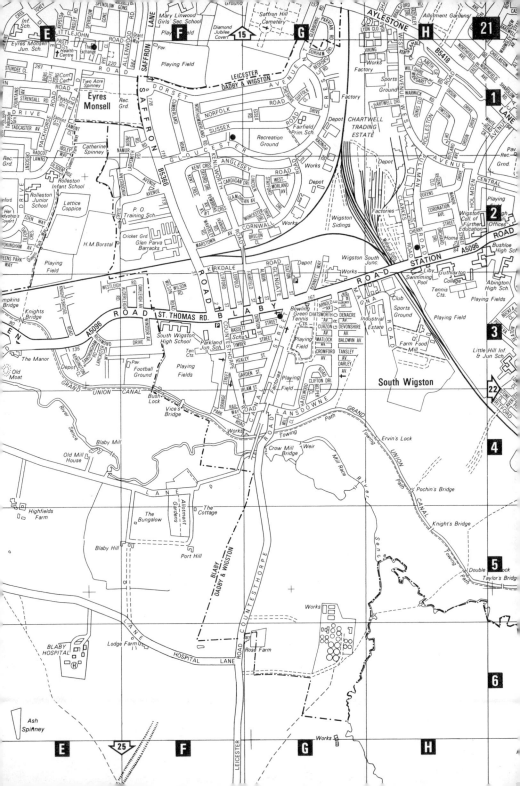

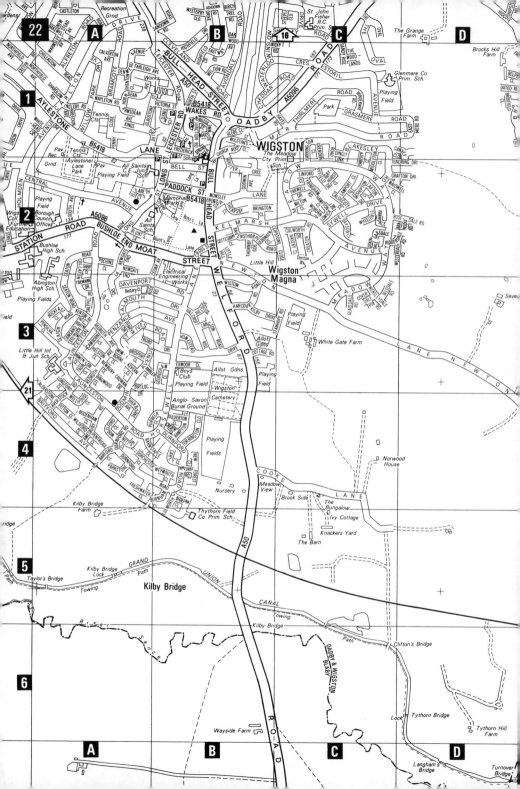

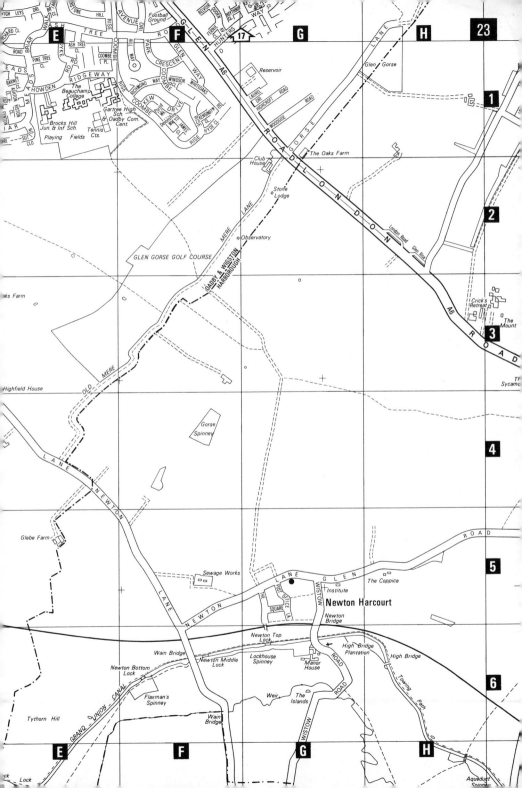

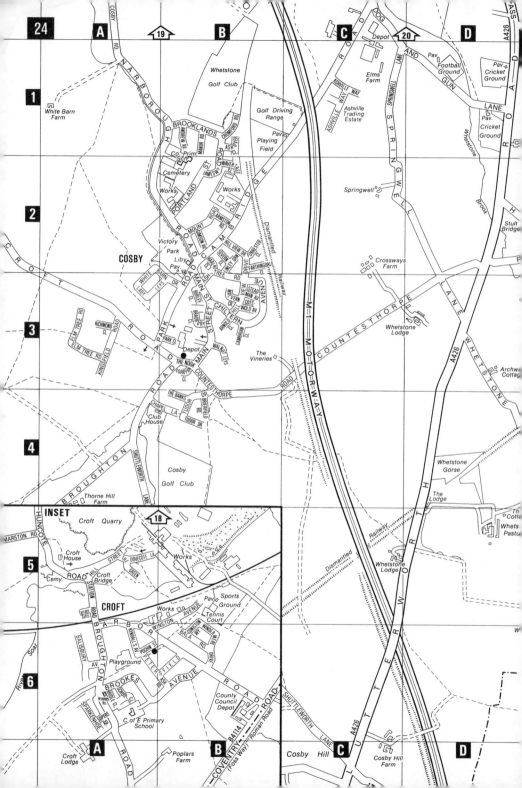

A ⬆19 B C ⬆20 D A426

1

White Barn Farm

Whetstone Golf Club

Golf Driving Range

Pav Playing Field

Depot

Elms Farm

Ashville Way

Ashville Trading Estate

Pav Football Ground

Pav Cricket Ground

Pav Cricket Ground

NARBOROUGH

BROOKLANDS

PRIMTHORPE RD

Co Prim Sch

MANOR RD

ANDREW ST

ST JAMES WY

ASTER

WAVERLEY

AVENUE

SPRINGWELL

DOG AND GUN LANE

2

COSBY

Cemetery

Works

Works

Victory Park

Libry Pav

PORTLAND

MOUNT ROAD

WHITE BARN DR

LADY LEYS DR

ARMSTON RD

HILL VIEW DR

SEVERN

FORBESTER DRIVE

TREE RD

FARTHINGDALE CL

STEAD MAN AV COTS WOLD AV

DRIVE

VIEW

MALVERN

MINTO

ARNOLD CL

CAMBRIAN CL

CHILTERN

MAIN ST

CROFT

Springwell

Crossways Farm

COUNTESTHORPE LANE

Whetstone Lodge

A426

Stult Bridge

Brook

WHETSTONE LANE

3

RICHMOND CL

ELM TREE RD

KINGSFIELD

ELM TREE RD

PARK RD

Park Cl

Depot

THE NOOK

FURZE CL

THE BANKS

MAIN ST

COUNTESTHORPE

TUDOR RD

BRIERFIELD DR

WALNUT LEYS

The Vineries

Road

Archwell Cottage

4

BROUGHTON

SHUTTLEWORTH LANE

CHAPEL LA

Club House

TUDOR DR

Cosby Golf Club

Whetstone Gorse

The Lodge

Whetstone Lodge

MI MOTORWAY

LUTTERWORTH

Railway

Dismantled

Th Cottage

Whets Pasture

INSET

Thorne Hill Farm

⬆18

Croft Quarry

Croft House

Cemy

MARSTON RD

HUNCOTE ROAD

STATION HILL ROAD

STREET W

Croft Bridge

DOVECOTE LA

GREEN

Works

Works

Dismantled

Railway

Whetstone Lodge

5

CROFT

Terrace Cotts

SALISBURY AV

NARBOROUGH

BROUGHTON

WINSTON AVENUE

KENNALS RD

KINGSTON WY

PUCKIN RD

BALA RD

MINDELLE DR

DRIVE

Sports Ground

Pav

Tennis Court

A426

River Soar

6

BROOKES

SPARKENHOE

SOPRS RD

Playground

PETERSFIELD

AVENUE

County Council Depot

B4114

COVENTRY ROAD

(Foss Way) Roman Road

SHUTTLEWORTH LANE

A

Croft Lodge

B

Poplars Farm

Cosby Hill

C

Cosby Hill Farm

D

C of E Primary School

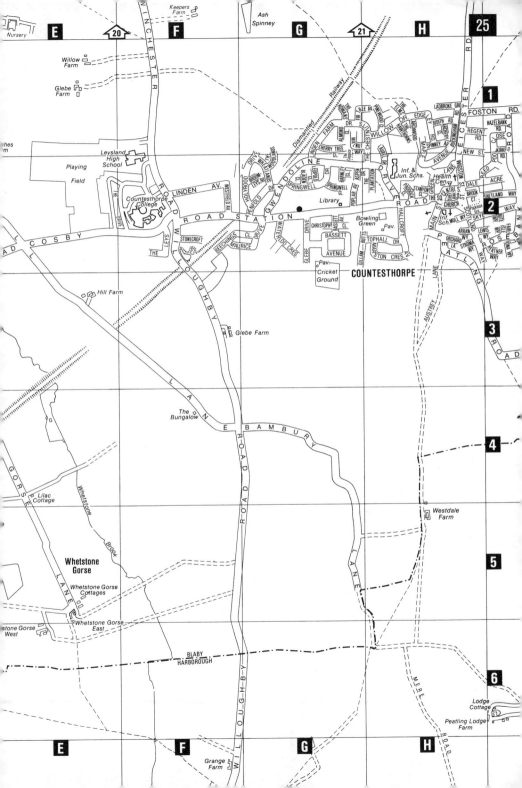

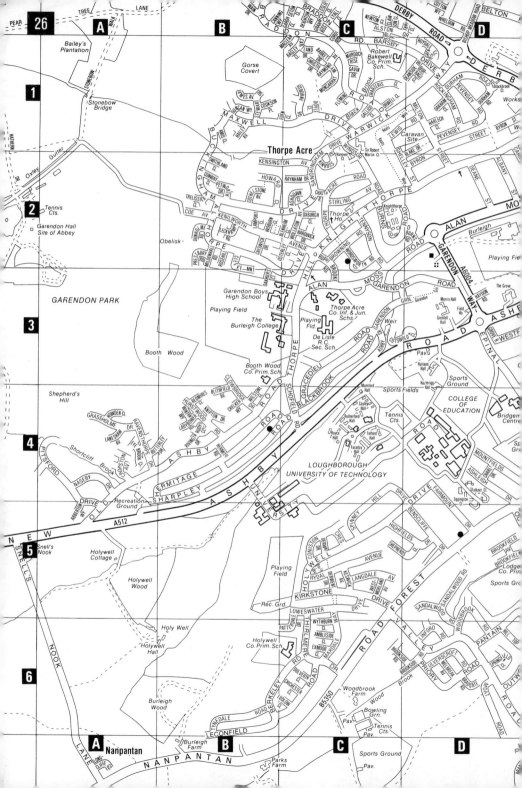

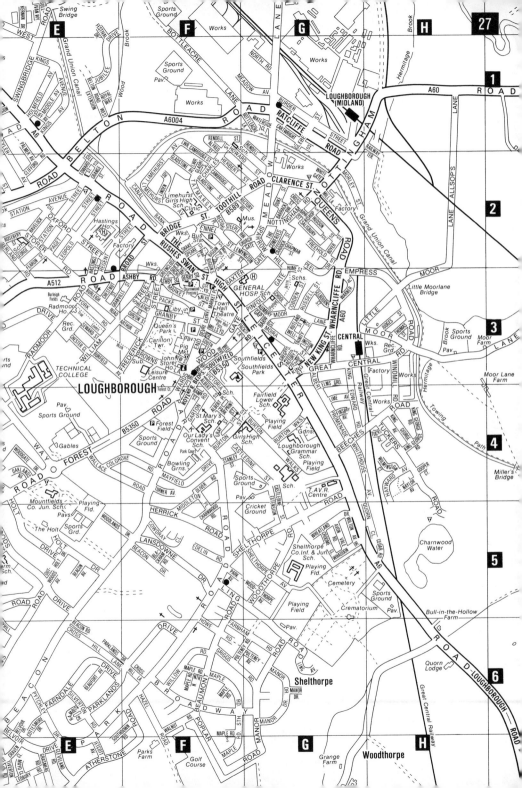

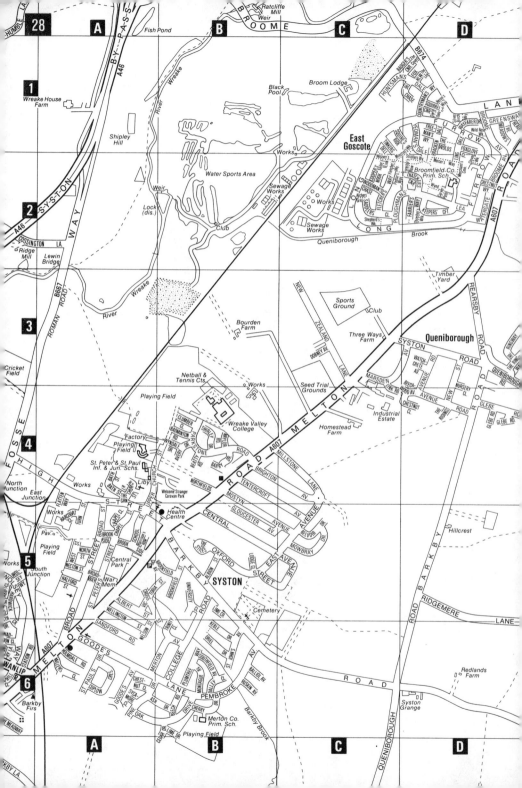

LARGE SCALE PLAN OF CITY CENTRE

Scale 6" to 1 mile

INDEX TO STREETS

HOW TO USE THIS INDEX

(a) A strict alphabetical order is followed in which Av., Rd., St., etc. are read in full and as part of the name preceding them; e.g. Abbotsford Rd. follows Abbots Clo. but precedes Abbots Rd.

(b) Each street is followed by its Postal Code District Number and map reference; e.g. Abberton Way. LE11—5A 26 is in the Leicester 11 Postal Code District and is to be found in square 5A on page 26.

N.B. The Postal Code District Numbers given in this index are, in fact, only the first part of the Postcode to each address and are only meant to indicate the Postal Code District in which each street is situated.

ABBREVIATIONS USED IN THIS INDEX

All : Alley	Chyd : Churchyard	Embkmt : Embankment	La : Lane	Pal : Palace	Sta : Station
App : Approach	Cir : Circus	Est : Estate	LE : Leicester	Pde : Parade	St : Street
Arc : Arcade	Clo : Close	Gdns : Gardens	Lit : Little	Pk : Park	Ter : Terrace
Av : Avenue	Comn : Common	Ga : Gate	Lwr : Lower	Pas : Passage	Up : Upper
Bk : Back	Cotts : Cottages	Gt : Great	Mans : Mansions	Pl : Place	Vs : Villas
Boulevd : Boulevard	Ct : Court	Grn : Green	Mkt : Market	Prom : Promenade	Wlk : Walk
Bri : Bridge	Cres : Crescent	Gro : Grove	M : Mews	Rd : Road	W : West
B'way : Broadway	Dri : Drive	Ho : House	Mt : Mount	S : South	Yd : Yard
Bldgs : Buildings	E : East	Junct : Junction	N : North	Sq : Square	

Abberton Way. LE11—5A 26
Abbeycourt Rd. LE4—5B 4
Abbey Dri. LE4—5B 4
Abbey Ga. LE4—2E 9
Abbey Ho. LE3—1C 8
Abbey La. LE4—1F 9 to 4C 4
Abbey Meadows. LE4—1F 9
Abbeymead Rd. LE4—5B 4
Abbey Pk. Rd. LE4—2E 9
Abbey Pk. St. LE4—2G 9
Abbey Rise. LE4—5B 4
Abbey Rd. LE9—3H 19
Abbey St. LE1—3G 9
Abbots Clo. LE5—1E 11
Abbotsford Rd. LE5—2D 10
Abbots Rd. LE5—1E 11
Aberdale Rd. LE7—5A 28
Aber Rd. LE2—1B 16
Aber Wlk. LE2—1B 16
Abingdon Rd. LE2—6H 9
Abney St. LE5—3A 10
Acacia Av. LE4—1D 4
Acan Way. LE9—5E 19
Acer Clo. LE4—4H 3
Acorn St. LE4—4D 4
Acres Rd. LE3—6E 7
Acton St. LE1—3G 9
Adcock Rd. LE3—3C 8
Adderley Rd. LE2—1H 15
Adlington Rd. LE2—4F 17
Agar St. LE4—6D 4
Aigburth. LE2—3D 16
Aikman Av. LE3—2A 8
Aikman Clo. LE3—1D 20
Ainsdale Rd. LE3—4B 8
Ainsworth Wlk. LE3—5E 9
Aintree Clo. LE5—5G 11
Aintree Cres. LE2—5C 16
Aisne Rd. LE8—1F 21
Alan Clo. LE4—4D 4
Alan Moss Rd. LE11—3C 26 to 2E 27
Albany St. LE11—2D 26
Albemarle Hall. LE5—1D 10
Alberta St. LE3—3H 9
Albert Pl. LE11—4F 27
Albert Rd. LE2—1A 16
Albert St. LE7—5A 28
Albert St. LE11—3F 21
Albion St. LE1—4G 9
Albion St. LE2—5E 17
Albion St. LE7—2D 2 (Anstey)
Albion St. LE7—5B 28 (Syston)
Albion St. LE8—3G 21
Alcester Dri. LE5—5G 11
Aldeby Clo. LE2—6C 14
Aldeby Clo. LE9—2A 20
Alderleigh Rd. LE2—1E 23
Alderstone Clo. LE8—4A 22
Alderton Clo. LE4—4H 3
Aldgate Av. LE5—6E 11
Alexander Av. LE9—1F 19

Alexander St. LE3—3E 9
Alexandra Ct. LE2—5E 17
Alexandra Rd. LE2—2B 16
Alexandra St. LE4—1G 5
Alexandra St. LE9—4G 19
Alfred Pl. LE1—4G 9
Alfred St. LE11—1F 27
Alfreton Rd. LE8—1A 22
Alice St. LE3—2E 9
Allandale Rd. LE2—1B 16
Allenwood Rd. LE2—1F 21
Allexton Gdns. LE5—2F 11
Alliance Rd. LE3—2G 7
Allington Dri. LE4—1D 4
Allington St. LE4—1H 9
Allinson Clo. LE5—3E 11
Alloway Clo. LE4—4F 5
All Saints Open. LE1—3F 9
All Saints Rd. LE3—3E 9
Allsop's La. LE11—1H 27
Alma St. LE3—3D 8
Almond Clo. LE8—1G 25
Almond Rd. LE2—6F 9
Alston Dri. LE11—2B 26
Althorpe Dri. LE11—2B 26
Alton Rd. LE2—5E 15
Alvaston Rd. LE3—2C 14
Alvecote Rd. LE2—1G 19
Amanda Rd. LE2—6C 14
Ambassador Rd. LE5—3D 10
Ambassador Wlk. LE4—4E 11
Ambergate Dri. LE4—1C 4
Amberley Clo. LE4—3H 3
Ambler Clo. LE8—3A 22
Ambleside Clo. LE2—1D 20
Ambleside Clo. LE11—6C 26
Ambleside Dri. LE2—1D 20
Ambleside Way. LE2—1D 20
Ambrose Clo. LE3—3C 8
Amersham Rd. LE4—1E 9
Amesbury Rd. LE8—4A 22
Amhurst Clo. LE3—1B 8
Amis Clo. LE11—1B 26
Amos Rd. LE3—4H 7
Amyson Rd. LE5—2F 11
Amy St. LE3—3C 14
Anchor St. LE4—6B 4
Andover St. LE2—5H 9
Andrew Av. LE9—1B 24
Andrewes Clo. LE3—4E 9
Andrewes St. LE3—4E 9
Andrew Rd. LE7—2E 3
Aneford Rd. LE4—6F 5
Angela Dri. LE5—5E 11
Angel Yd. LE11—3F 27
Anglesey Rd. LE8—2F 21
Angus Clo. LE7—4H 11
Ann St. LE1—4G 9
Ann's Way. LE2—6F 17
Anstey Clo. LE4—3 to 1E 9
Anstey La. LE6—5B 2
Anstey La. LE3—3H 7
Anthony Dri. LE7—4H 11
Anthony Rd. LE4—6A 4
Apollo Clo. LE2—4H 9
Applegate. LE1—4F 9

Appleton Av. LE4—4A 4
Approach, The. LE5—5C 10
Arbor Rd. LE9—6A 24
Arbour Rd. LE4—6D 4
Arcade, The. LE8—1B 22
Archdeacon La. LE1—2G 9
Archer Clo. LE4—4F 5
Archery Clo. LE8—1H 25
Archway Rd. LE5—1G 11
Ardath Rd. LE4—1A 10
Arden Av. LE3—1B 14
Arden Ter. LE3—1C 14
Armadale Dri. LE5—2F 11
Armadale Grn. LE5—2F 11
Armson Av. LE9—4C 6
Armston Rd. LE9—2B 24
Arncliffe Rd. LE5—1F 11
Arnesby Cres. LE2—5F 15
Arnhem St. LE1—5G 9
Arnold Av. LE8—3G 21
Arnold Clo. LE9—3B 24
Arran Rd. LE4—4E 5
Arran Way. LE8—2F 25
Arreton Clo. LE2—4A 16
Arthur St. LE11—3F 27
Arum Way. LE3—4H 7
Arundel St. LE3—4D 8
Ascot Rd. LE4—6D 4
Asfordby St. LE5—3B 10
Ashburne Rd. LE8—6A 16
Ashbourne St. LE4—4A 10
Ashby Cres. LE11—3C 26
Ashby Rd. LE11—3D 26 to 3F 27
Ashby Sq. LE11—3F 27
Ash Clo. LE6—1A 6
Ashclose Av. LE2—4A 16
Ashdown Av. LE3—4C 8
Ashdown Clo. LE11—2C 26
Ashdown Rd. LE8—6B 16
Ash Dri. LE7—6B 28
Ashfield St. LE7—3D 2
Ashfield Rd. LE2—6A 10
Ashfield Rd. LE4—1H 5
Ashford Rd. LE2—2G 15
Ash Gro. LE8—4C 20
Ashington Clo. LE3—1C 8
Ashleigh Rd. LE11—4D 26
Ashleigh Rd. LE3—1G 7 (Glenfield)
Ashleigh Rd. LE3—6D 8 (Leicester centre)
Ashlyns Rise. LE3—5H 7
Ashover Clo. LE8—4A 24
Ashover Rd. LE5—5A 10
Ash St. LE5—2A 10
Ashton Clo. LE2—1E 23
Ashton Clo. LE8—3A 22
Ash Tree Clo. LE2—1E 23
Ash Tree Rd. LE2—6E 17
Ash Tree Rd. LE8—3B 10
Ashurst Rd. LE3—3A 14
Ashville Trading Est. LE4—1C 24
Ashville Way. LE8—1C 24

Ashwell St. LE1—5G 9
Aspen Dri. LE8—2G 25
Asplin Rd. LE2—5F 15
Asquith Boulevd. LE2—5G 15
Astill Dri. LE4—4B 4
Astill Lodge Rd. LE4—2F 3
Astley Clo. LE3—6C 8
Aston Hill. LE2—3G 15
Atherstone Clo. LE2—6F 17
Atherstone Rd. LE11—6E 27
Atkinson St. LE5—3B 10
Atkins St. LE2—4H 9
Atlas Clo. LE2—4H 9
Attfield Dri. LE8—5B 20
Attingham Clo. LE4—1B 10
Auburn Ho. LE3—2B 8
Auburn Rd. LE8—4C 20
Auden Clo. LE6—5G 3
Audley End. LE3—2C 14
Aumberry Gap. LE11—3G 27
Austin Rise. LE5—1F 11
Austrey La. LE8—3H 25
Austwick Clo. LE4—5H 3
Avebury Av. LE4—1D 8
Avenue Gdns. LE2—2A 16
Avenue Rd. LE2—2A 16
Avenue Rd. LE7—4D 28
Avenue Rd. Extension. LE2—2H 15
Avenue, The. LE2—1A 16
Avenue, The. LE3—1G 7
Avenue, The. LE8—4C 20
Averil Rd. LE5—3E 11
Avery Dri. LE7—4B 28
Avery Hill. LE5—5H 7
Avoca Clo. LE5—3E 11
Avon Clo. LE2—4F 9
Avondale Rd. LE8—1B 22
Avon Dri. LE8—5A 20
Avon Rd. LE3—1A 14
Avonside Dri. LE5—4D 10
Avon St. LE2—5H 9
Avon Vale Rd. LE11—5G 27
Axbridge Clo. LE4—1E 9
Aylestone Dri. LE2—5E 15
Aylestone La. LE8—6H 15
Aylestone Rd. LE2—4D 14 to 6F 9
Aylmer Rd. LE3—5B 8
Aysgarth Rd. LE4—5H 3
Ayston Rd. LE3—2B 14
Babingley Dri. LE4—6A 4
Babington Row. LE2—5H 9
Baddeley Dri. LE8—6H 15
Baden Rd. LE5—2B 10
Badgers Clo. LE4—5G 3
Badger's Corner. LE7—1D 28
Badminton Rd. LE4—4F 5
Badminton Rd. LE7—4B 28
Baggrave St. LE5—3B 10
Bagley Clo. LE11—1C 26
Bainbridge Rd. LE3—2C 14
Baines La. LE8—6F 7
Bakewell Rd. LE8—5A 16
Bakewell St. LE2—4A 10
Barry Clo. LE3—6D 8

Bala Rd. LE9—6B 24
Balcombe Av. LE3—3C 8
Balderstone Clo. LE5—4D 10
Baldwin Av. LE8—3G 21
Baldwin Rd. LE2—5H 15
Bale Rd. LE4—1B 10
Balfour St. LE3—2E 9
Balisfire Gro. LE4—5G 3
Balk, The. LE3—1G 7
Balladine Rd. LE7—1E 3
Ballards Clo. LE4—5G 3
Ballater Clo. LE5—6G 11
Balliol Av. LE7—6B 28
Balmoral Dri. LE3—1A 14
Bambury La. LE8—4G 25
Bambury Way. LE2—4G 15
Bampton Clo. LE8—4B 22
Bampton St. LE11—4F 27
Bankart Av. LE2—2C 16
Bankside. LE5—2G 11
Banks Rd. LE2—4E 15
Banks, The. LE8—4D 10
Bank, The. LE2—2H 25
Bannerman Rd. LE5—6B 10
Bantlam La. LE9—1F 19
Barbara Av. LE3—4B 8
Barbara Av. LE5—2E 11
Barbara Clo. LE9—1E 19
Barbara Rd. LE3—2C 14
Barclay St. LE3—5D 8
Bardolph St. LE4—1H 9
Bardolph St. E. LE4—1H 9
Barfoot Rd. LE2—6G 15
Barford Clo. LE8—4A 22
Baringate Clo. LE4—4A 4
Barkby La. LE7—6A 28
Barkby Rd. LE4—6F to 4G 5
Barkby Rd. LE7—5D 28 (Queniborough)
Barkby Rd. LE7—5B 28 (Syston)
Barkbythorpe Rd. LE4—4H 5
Barker St. LE3—3A 10
Barkford Clo. LE4—1H 11
Barmouth Av. LE2—5G 15
Barnard Clo. LE4—4H 9
Barnard Wlk. LE4—4H 9
Barnby Av. LE8—6A 16
Barnes Clo. LE4—3G 5
Barnes Heath Rd. LE5—4D 10
Barnet Clo. LE2—1E 23
Barnley Clo. LE8—2G 25
Barns Clo. LE8—4B 6
Barnsdale Rd. LE4—5H 3
Barnstaple Clo. LE8—4A 22
Barnstaple Rd. LE5—6F 11
Barnwell Av. LE4—4B 4
Baronet Way. LE5—1G 11
Baron St. LE1—4G 9
Barrack Row. LE11—2G 27
Barratt Clo. LE2—1A 16
Barrett Dri. LE11—1C 26
Barrington Rd. LE2—2C 16
Barrow La. LE3—1F 7
Barrow St. LE11—3G 27
Barry Clo. LE3—6D 8

Barry Rd. LE3—6C 6
Barry Dri. LE7—4B 28
Barry Rd. LE5—1G 11
Barsby Dri. LE11—1C 26
Barsby Wlk. LE4—4A 4
Barshaw Rd. LE4—3H 3
Barston St. LE1—3F 9
Bartholomew St. LE2—5A 10
Barton Clo. LE8—3A 22
Barton Rd. LE3—2D 8
Barwell Rd. LE9—4C 6
Baslow Rd. LE5—5A 10
Bassett Av. LE2—2G 25
Bassett St. LE3—3A 9
Bassett St. LE8—3F 21
Bateman Rd. LE3—2A 8
Bath La. LE3 & LE1—4E 9
Bath St. LE4—5C & 4D 4
Bath St. LE7—4A 28
Bathurst Rd. LE5—5G 11
Battenburg Rd. LE3—3D 8
Batten St. LE2—2C 15
Battersbee Rd. LE3—1A 8
Battersbee Rd. LE3—1A 8
Battersbee Way. LE3—1A 8
Baxter Ga. LE11—3F 27
Baxters Clo. LE4—5G 3
Baycliff Clo. LE3—1C 8
Bayham Clo. LE5—1A 8
Baysdale. LE8—2C 22
Bay St. LE1—3F 9
Beacon Av. LE4—1G 5
Beacon Av. LE11—5E 27
Beacon Rd. LE11—5F 27
Beaconsfield Rd. LE3—5D 8
Beal St. LE2—4H 9
Beatrice Rd. LE3—2C 8
Beatty Av. LE5—3C 10
Beatty Rd. LE5—3C 10
Beatty Rd. LE7—4B 28
Beaufort Av. LE11—6E 27
Beaufort Rd. LE3—2C 14
Beaumanor Rd. LE4—5B 4
Beaumont Hall. LE2—3C 16
Beaumont Leys La. LE4—5A 4
Beaumont Leys La. LE4—2H 3 to 6B 4
Beaumont Rd. LE5—3A 10
Beaumont Rd. LE11—6F 27
Beaumont St. LE2—4D 16
Beaumont Wlk. LE4—5F to 5H 3
Beauville Dri. LE4—5G 3
Beck Clo. LE2—4D 16
Beckett Rd. LE5—1C 10
Beckingham Rd. LE2—6A 10
Bedale Dri. LE4—3H 3
Bede St. LE3—5E 9
Bedford Rd. LE8—1G 21
Bedford Sq. LE11—3F 27
Bedford St. LE11—3F 27
Bedford St. N. LE1—3G 9
Bedford St. S. LE1—3G 9
Beeby Rd. LE5—3B 10
Beeby Rd. LE7—1H & 2H 11
Beechcroft Av. LE3—2C 14

Beechcroft Rd. LE2—2A 16
Beech Dri. LE3—1G 13
Beeches Rd. LE1—4G 27
Beechfield Av. LE4—2C 4
Beechings Clo. LE8—2F 25
Beech Rd. LE2—6D 16
Beech Rd. LE7—6B 28
Beech Rd. LE8—5C 20
Beech St. LE5—2A 10
Beechwood Av. LE3—6E 7
Beechwood Av. LE4—2F 5
Beechwood Av. LE7—4D 28
Beechwood Clo. LE5—4F 11
Beechwood Rd. LE9—6F 19
Bee Hive La. LE11—3F 27
Beggar's La. LE3 & LE9—1D 12 to 6E 13
Belgrave Av. LE4—5C 4
Belgrave Boulevd. LE4—3H 3 & 4B 4
Belgrave Circle. LE1—2G 9
Belgrave Flyover. LE1—2G 9
Belgrave Ga. LE1—3G 9 (in two parts)
Belgrave Rd. LE4—1G 9
Bell Clo. LE6—1B 6
Bellville Dri. LE2—5F 17
Bell Vue. LE9—4G 19
Bell Vue Av. LE4—6B 4
Bellholme Clo. LE4—5D 4
Bell La. LE5—3H 9
Bell La. LE9—4G 19
Bell St. LE8—2B 22
Belmont St. LE2—4E 15
Belper Clo. LE2—1D 22
Belper Clo. LE8—4G 21
Belper St. LE4—1H 9
Belton Clo. LE2—5F 15
Belton Rd. LE3—2B 14
Belton Rd. LE11—1E 27
Belton Rd. W. LE11—1D 26
Belton Rd. W. Extension. LE11—1E 27
Belvoir Clo. LE2—6F 17
Belvoir Dri. LE2—4D 14
Belvoir Dri. LE7—5C 28
Belvoir Dri. LE11—6E 27
Belvoir Dri. E. LE2—5E 15
Belvoir St. LE1—4G 9
Beman Clo. LE4—3G 5
Bembridge Clo. LE3—2D 8
Bembridge Rd. LE3—1D 8
Bencroft Clo. LE7—2D 2
Bendbow Rise. LE3—6H 7 to 6A 8
Bennett Rise. LE9—4C 18
Bennett Wlk. LE3—5B 8
Bennett Way. LE8—3G 21
Bennion Rd. LE4—4F to 2H 3
Benscliffe Dri. LE11—5D 26
Benscliffe Gdns. LE2—1E 21
Benskin Wlk. LE4—6G 3
Benson St. LE5—4C 10
Bentburn Ho. LE3—2B 8
Bentinghouse Gdns. LE2—6E 15
Bentinghouse Rd. LE2—6E 15
Bentley Rd. LE4—1C 4
Beresford Dri. LE2—3B 16
Berkeley Clo. LE2—6G 17
Berkeley Rd. LE11—6B 26
Berkley St. LE1—3F 9
Berkshire Rd. LE2—4E 15
Berners St. LE2—4H 9
Berridge Dri. LE2—6E 17
Berridge La. LE4—5D 4
Berridge St. LE1—4F 9
Berrington Clo. LE5—2B 10
Berry's La. LE6—1B 6
Beverley Av. LE4—1H 9
Beverley Clo. LE4—1G 5
Bevington Clo. LE6—1B 6
Bewcastle Gro. LE4—3A 4
Bewcastle Ho. LE4—3A 4
Bewicke Rd. LE3—1C 14
Bexhill Rise. LE5—2H 11
Biam Way. LE3—3B 14
Biddle Rd. LE3—2C 8
Biddle Rd. LE9—5G 19
Biddulph Av. LE2—5A 10
Biddulph St. LE2—5A 10
Bideford Clo. LE8—5B 22
Bideford Rd. LE5—6G 11
Bidford Clo. LE3—1A 14
Bidford Ct. LE3—1A 14
Bidford Rd. LE3—1A 14
Biggin Hill Rd. LE5—1E 17
Biggin St. LE11—2F 27
Bignal Dri. LE3—6F 7
Bilberry Clo. LE3—4B 14
Billington Clo. LE4—5A 4
Bilsdale Rd. LE8—3C 22
Bingley Rd. LE9—5G 19
Birch Clo. LE4—1B 10
Birchtree Rd. LE8—6B 16
Birds Nest Av. LE3—1B 8
Birkdale Av. LE2—2A 16
Birkdale Rd. LE7—2C 2
Birkenshaw Clo. LE3—1B 8
Birsmore Av. LE4—4F 5
Birstall Rd. LE4—4C to 2D 4
Birstall St. LE1—2H 9
Birstow Cres. LE4—3A 4
Bishopdale Rd. LE4—5H 3
Bishop Meadow Rd. LE11—1D 26
Bishopston Wlk. LE4—4B 4
Bishop St. LE1—4G 9
Bishop St. LE11—2G 27
Bisley St. LE3—6E 9
Blaby By-Pass. LE8—5B 20
Blaby Rd. LE8—3F 21
Blaby Rd. LE9—1F to 2H 19
Blackbird Av. LE4—1E 9
Blackbird Rd. LE4—2E 9
Blackbrook Ct. LE11—1D 26
Blackbrook Rd. LE11—4C 26
Blackett Av. LE3—2C 8
Blackfriars St. LE3—4E 9
Blackham Rd. LE11—5F 27
Blackmore Dri. LE3—5B 8
Blackthorn La. LE2—4E 17
Bladen Clo. LE8—2G 25
Blaise Gro. LE4—1B 10
Blake Ct. LE9—1E 19
Blake Dri. LE11—1D 26
Blakenhall Rd. LE5—4D 10
Blakesley Rd. LE8—1C 22
Blakesley Wlk. LE4—6G 3
Blake St. LE1—3F 9
Bland Rd. LE3—1A 8
Blankley Dri. LE2—2B 16
Blanklyn Av. LE5—4B 10
Blaydon Clo. LE3—1C 8
Blenheim Clo. LE11—2C 26
Blenheim Rd. LE4—1D 4
Blenheim Way. LE4—4A 4
Blickling Wlk. LE5—2B 10
Blissett Rd. LE3—2C 8
Blithfield Av. LE11—4B 26
Bloomfield Rd. LE2—4F 15
Blount Rd. LE4—2H 5
Bloxham Rd. LE3—2C 8
Blue Banks Av. LE2—2B 20
Blue Gates Rd. LE4—3F 3
Blundell Rd. LE5—6D 10
Blunt's La. LE8—2A 22
Bodenham Clo. LE8—4A 22
Bodkin Wlk. LE4—5G 3
Bodmin Av. LE8—4A 22
Bodnant Av. LE5—6B 10
Bollington Rd. LE2—5F 17
Bolsover St. LE5—4B 10
Bolton Rd. LE3—4D 8
Bonchurch St. LE3—3E 9
Bondman Clo. LE4—4B 4
Bonners La. LE2—5F 9
Bonney Rd. LE3—1B 8
Bonnington Rd. LE2—2H 15
Bonsall St. LE5—5A 10
Bonville Pl. LE3—2C 14
Booth Clo. LE5—4E 11
Border Dri. LE4—3A 4
Borlace St. LE3—3D 8
Borrowdale Way. LE5—6G 11
Borrowdale Way. LE11—5C 26
Boston Rd. LE4—4F 3
Boswell St. LE9—3E 19
Bosworth St. LE3—4D 8
Botley Wlk. LE5—3D 10
Bottleacre La. LE11—1F & 1G 27
Boulder La. LE2—4G 15
Boulter Cres. LE8—2B 22
Boundary Rd. LE2—2E 15
Bourton Cres. LE2—5F 17
Bow Bri. St. LE3—4E 9
Bowhill Gro. LE5—3G 11
Bowling Grn. St. LE1—4F 9
Bowmar's La. LE3—3E 9
Boyer St. LE11—2G 27
Boyers Wlk. LE3—6E 7
Brabazon Rd. LE2—4D 16
Bracken Dale. LE7—1D 28
Brackenfield Way. LE4—1H 5
Brackenthwaite. LE4—5F 5
Brackley Clo. LE4—1B 10
Bradbourne Rd. LE5—5B 10
Bradbury Clo. LE9—3B 24
Braddon Rd. LE11—1B 26
Bradfield Clo. LE5—5C 10
Bradgate Av. LE4—1G 5
Bradgate Dri. LE4—4F 3
Bradgate Dri. LE6—1B 6
Bradgate Dri. LE8—6H 15
Bradgate Rd. LE7—2C 2
Bradgate Rd. LE11—6D 26
Bradgate St. LE4—2E 9
Brading Rd. LE3—2D 8
Bradshaw Av. LE2—1D 20
Bradstone Rd. LE2—5E 15
Braemar Clo. LE4—4E 5
Braemar Dri. LE4—4E 5
Brailsford Rd. LE3—4A 8
Brailsford Rd. LE8—6H 15
Bramall Rd. LE5—2B 10
Bramber Clo. LE4—3F 5
Bramble Way. LE3—2B 14
Brambling Rd. LE5—3A 10
Brambling Way. LE2—6D 16
Bramcote Rd. LE3—2C 14
Bramcote Rd. LE8—1A 22
Bramcote Rd. LE11—6D 26
Bramley Rd. LE3—4D 8
Bramley Rd. LE4—1D 4
Brampton Av. LE3—4C 8
Brampton Way. LE2—5C 16
Brancaster Clo. LE4—6H 3
Brandon St. LE4—1H 9
Bransdale Rd. LE8—2D 22
Branting Hill. LE6—5B 2
Branting Hill Av. LE3—6B 2
Branting Hill Gro. LE3—5B 2
Braunstone Av. LE3—1B 14 to 5D 8
Braunstone Clo. LE3—2B 14
Braunstone Ga. LE3—5E 9
Braunstone La. LE3—6G 7 to 2C 14
Braunstone La. E. LE3—3C 14
Braybrooke Rd. LE4—1B 10
Brazil St. LE2—6F 9
Brecon Clo. LE8—2G 21
Breedon Av. LE8—1A 22
Breedon St. LE2—4A 10
Brent Knowle Gdns. LE5—4G 11
Brentwood Rd. LE2—2G 15
Bretby Rd. LE2—5E 15
Brettell Rd. LE2—6E 15
Bretton Clo. LE4—5B 4
Bretton Wlk. LE4—5B 4
Brewer Clo. LE4—4G 5
Brex Rise. LE3—3H 7
Brian Rd. LE4—1E 9
Brianway, The. LE5—3C 10
Briar Clo. LE2—6E 17
Briarfield Dri. LE5—1G 11
Briargate Dri. LE4—1B 4
Briar Meads. LE2—1E 23
Briar Rd. LE5—2G 11
Briar Wlk. LE2—1E 23
Bridevale Rd. LE2—5E 15
Bridge Rd. LE5—3B 10
Bridge St. LE11—2F 27
Bridgeway. LE8—5A 20
Bridle Clo. LE9—6A 24
Bridlespur Way. LE4—3B 4
Bridle, The. LE2—1C 20
Bridport Clo. LE8—3A 22
Brierfield Rd. LE9—4B 24
Brighton Av. LE7—4B 28
Brighton Av. LE8—6A 16
Brighton Rd. LE5—2B 10
Brightside Rd. LE5—6B 10
Bright St. LE1—3H 9
Brightwell Dri. LE3—5F 7
Brindley Rise. LE5—1H 11
Bringhurst Grn. LE3—2H 7
Bringhurst Rd. LE3—3H 7
Brington Clo. LE8—2B 22
Brinsmead Rd. LE2—4H 15
Bristol Av. LE4—1E 9
Britannia St. LE1—2G 9
Britford Av. LE8—4A 22
Briton St. LE3—5E 9
Brixham Dri. LE2 & LE8—6G 15
Brixworth Rise. LE5—3H 11
Broad Av. LE5—4C 10
Broadbent Clo. LE8—5B 20
Broadford Clo. LE4—4E 5
Broadgate Clo. LE4—1C 4
Broadhurst St. LE4—6D 4
Broadmead Rd. LE8—5B 20
Broad St. LE7—5A 28
Broad St. LE9—1F 19
Broad St. LE11—2F 27
Broadway. LE7—5A 28
Broadway. LE11—6F 27
Broadway Rd. LE5—1B 16
Broadway, The. LE2—2D 16
Brockenhurst Dri. LE3—3A 14
Brocklesby Way. LE5—1G 11
Brocks Hill Clo. LE2—6E 17
Brocks Hill Dri. LE2—6E 17
Brodick Wlk. LE5—2B 10
Bromhead St. LE11—2G 27
Brook Ct. LE8—2H 25
Brookdale Rd. LE3—4H 7
Brookes Av. LE9—6A 24
Brookes Ho. LE9—6A 24
Brookfield Av. LE7—5B 28
Brookfield Av. LE11—5D 26
Brookfield Rise. LE2—5G 15
Brookfield St. LE7—5B 28
Brook Gdns. LE2—1C 20
Brookhouse Av. LE2—5H 9
Brookhouse St. LE2—5H 9
Brookland Rd. LE2—2G 15
Brooklands Clo. LE8—5B 20
Brooklands Rd. LE9—1B 24
Brook Rd. LE5—3G 11
Brooksby Clo. LE2—5D 16
Brooksby Dri. LE2—5D 16
Brooksby St. LE2—2F 15
Brook Side. LE7—5A 28 (in two parts)
Brookside. LE8—5B 20
Brook Side. LE11—3F 27
Brookside Dri. LE2—5F 17
Brookside Rd. LE11—6D 26
Brook St. LE4—1F 5
Brook St. LE7—5A 28
Brook St. LE8—5B 20
Brook St. LE9—1F 19 (Enderby)
Brook St. LE9—5C 18 (Huncote)
Broome Av. LE7—1D 28
Broome La. LE7—1B 28
Broomleys. LE8—2G 25
Brougham St. LE1—3H 9
Broughton Rd. LE2—5F 15
Broughton Rd. LE9—4A 24 (Cosby)
Broughton Rd. LE9—6A 24 (Croft)
Browning Rd. LE11—2C 26
Browning St. LE3—5D 8
Browning St. LE9—3E 19
Browns La. LE11—3F 27 (in two parts)
Broxburn Clo. LE4—4F 5
Broxfield Clo. LE2—1D 22
Bruce St. LE3—6E 9
Bruin St. LE4—6C 4
Bruins Wlk. LE2—5D 16
Brunel Av. LE3—1C 8
Brunswick St. LE1—3H 9
Bryngarth Cres. LE5—3E 11
Buchan Wlk. LE3—5B 8
Buckfast Clo. LE5—6C 10
Buckfast Clo. LE8—3A 22
Buckhaven Clo. LE4—4F 5
Buckingham Dri. LE11—2B 26
Buckingham Rd. LE8—1H 25
Buckland Rd. LE5—1B 10
Buckminster Rd. LE3—1D 8
Bucksburn Wlk. LE4—4E 5
Bude Dri. LE3—1G 7
Bude Rd. LE8—3A 22
Buller Rd. LE4—1G 9
Bull Head St. LE8—1B to 2B 22
Bulwer Rd. LE2—2H 15 (in two parts)
Burder St. LE11—1G 27
Burdet Clo. LE3—2A 14
Burdett Way. LE4—4A 4
Burfield Av. LE11—3E 27
Burfield St. LE4—1H 9
Burgess Rd. LE2—4E 15
Burgess St. LE1—3F 9
Burgess St. LE8—1B 22
Burgin Rd. LE7—3C 2
Burleigh Av. LE8—6H 15
Burleigh Fields. LE11—3E 27
Burleigh Rd. LE11—3E 27
Burley Clo. LE9—3B 24
Burleys Flyover. LE1—3G 9
Burleys Way. LE1—3F 9
Burlington Rd. LE2—2A 16
Burnaby Av. LE5—3A 10
Burnaston Rd. LE2—5E 15
Burnell Rd. LE3—1C 14
Burnham Clo. LE8—4B 22
Burnham Dri. LE4—6A 4
Burnmoor St. LE2—1F 15
Burnside Rd. LE2—5G 15
Burns Rd. LE11—2C 26
Burns St. LE2—3G 15
Burns St. LE9—3F 19
Burrage Clo. LE11—1D 26
Burroughs Rd. LE6—1B 6
Bursdon Clo. LE3—3H 7
Bursom Rd. LE4—2G 3
Burton Clo. LE2—6F 17
Burton St. LE1—4G 9
Burtonn St. LE11—4F 27
Burton Walks. LE11—4G 27
Buscot Clo. LE4—1B 10
Bushby Rd. LE5—2B 10
Bushloe End. LE8—2A 22
Butcombe Rd. LE4—1E 9
Bute Way. LE8—2H 25
Butler Clo. LE4—4G 5
Butt Clo. La. LE1—3F 9
Butterley Dri. LE11—4A 26
Buttermere St. LE2—6F 9
Butterwick Dri. LE4—4H 3
Buxton Clo. LE8—5B 20
Buxton St. LE2—4A 10
Byfield Dri. LE8—2C 22
Byford Rd. LE4—6B 4
Byron Clo. LE9—2F 19
Byron St. LE1—3G 9
Byron St. LE11—2D 26
Byron St. Extension. LE11—1D 26
Byway Rd. LE5—1B 16
Cademan Clo. LE2—3H 15
Cairnsford Rd. LE2—4H 15
Calais Hill. LE1—5G 9
Calais St. LE1—5G 9
Calcary Rd. LE1—2G 9
Caldecott Clo. LE8—2C 22
Caldecott Rd. LE3—2B 14
Calder Ho. LE2—1D 20
Calder Rd. LE4—5H 3
Caldwell St. LE11—3F 27
Caledine Rd. LE3—2B 8
Callan Clo. LE9—4F 19
Calver Hey Rd. LE4—5G 3
Calverton Av. LE8—1A 22
Calverton Clo. LE6—2B 6
Camborne Clo. LE8—3A 22
Cambrian Clo. LE9—3B 24
Cambridge Rd. LE9 & LE8—2B 24 to 5B 20
Cambridge St. LE3—5D 8
Cambridge St. LE11—2F 27
Camden Rd. LE3—2B 14
Camden St. LE1—3G 9
Cameron Av. LE4—5D 4
Camfield Rise. LE2—6E 15
Campbell Av. LE4—3G 5
Campbell St. LE1—4G 9
Campion Wlk. LE4—5G 3
Camville Rd. LE3—5B 8
Canal Bank. LE11—2F 27
Canal St. LE2—4D 14
Canal St. LE4—1F 5
Canal St. LE8—4G 21
Cank St. LE1—4F 9
Canning Pl. LE1—3F 9
Canning St. LE1—3F 9
Canning Way. LE11—1B 26
Cannock St. LE4—4H 5
Canon Clo. LE2—6E 17
Canonsleigh Rd. LE4—5B 4
Canonsleigh Wlk. LE4—5B 4
Canon St. LE4—6D 4
Canterbury Ter. LE3—6D 8
Cantrell Rd. LE3—6H 7
Canvey Clo. LE8—1C 22
Capers Clo. LE9—1E 19
Capesthorne Clo. LE5—2B 10
Carberry Clo. LE2—6G 17
Cardigan Dri. LE8—2F 21
Cardinal Clo. LE6—2B 6
Cardinals Wlk. LE5—2F 11
Carey Clo. LE8—4B 22
Carey Rd. LE9—5C 18
Carey's Clo. LE1—4F 9
Carfax Av. LE2—4C 16
Carington St. LE11—2D 26
Carisbrooke Av. LE2—3A 16
Carisbrooke Rd. LE2—3A 16
Carlisle St. LE3—4D 8
Carl St. LE2—5D 14
Carlton Av. LE9—4G 19
Carlton Dri. LE8—1A 22
Carlton St. LE1—5F 9
Carmen Gro. LE6—3A 2
Carnation St. LE4—5C 4
Carpe Rd. LE4—1B 10
Carrow Rd. LE3—5F 7
Carter Clo. LE9—1E 19
Carter St. LE4—1A 10
Cartland Dri. LE11—1C 26
Carts La. LE1—4F 9
Cartwright Dri. LE2—5D 16
Cartwright St. LE11—1G 27
Carver's Path. LE7—2D 28
Cashmore View. LE4—4H 3
Castell Dri. LE6—5A 2
Castledine St. LE11—4G 27
Castledine St. Extension. LE11 4G 27
Castle Fields. LE4—3F 3
Castleford Rd. LE3—3A 14
Castlegate Av. LE4—1C 4
Castle Rd. LE9—4C 6
Castle St. LE1—4F 9
Castleton Rd. LE8—6A 16
Castle View. LE1—4F 9
Castor Clo. LE2—4H 9
Caswell Clo. LE4—4A 4
Caters Clo. LE7—2D 2
Catesby St. LE3—4E 9
Catherine St. LE1 & LE4—2H 9 to 6F 5
Cathkin Clo. LE3—4H 7
Cattlemarket. LE11—3F 27
Causeway La. LE1—3F 9
Cavendish Rd. LE2—2F 15
Caversham Rd. LE2—1D 20
Cawsand Rd. LE8—3A 22
Cayley Hall. LE11—4C 26
Cecilia Rd. LE2—1H 15
Cecil Rd. LE2—3H 9
Cedar Av. LE4—1C 4
Cedar Av. LE8—2B 22
Cedar Clo. LE3—6D 2
Cedar Cres. LE9—4F 19
Cedar Dri. LE7—6B 28
Cedar Rd. LE2—5A 10
Cedar Rd. LE8—5C 20
Cedar Rd. LE11—5H 27
Cedars Ct. LE2—1A 16
Cedarwood Clo. LE4—1B 10
Celt St. LE3—5E 9
Cemetery Rd. LE8—4B 20
Central Av. LE2—1A 16
Central Av. LE7—5B 28
Central Av. LE8—2A 22
Central Clo. LE8—4A 20
Central Rd. LE3—2E 9
Central St. LE8—2G 25
Chadwell Rd. LE3—3H 7
Chadwick Wlk. LE4—5A 4
Chale Rd. LE4—6B 4
Chalgrove Wlk. LE5—3D 10
Chalvington Clo. LE5—6F 11

Champion Clo. LE5—4E 11
Chancery St. LE1—4F 9
Chandos St. LE2—5A 10
Chapel Clo. LE7—5A 28
Chapel Grn. LE3—6F 7
Chapel Hill. LE6—2B 2
Chapel La. LE2—3H 15
Chapel La. LE6—2B 6
Chapel La. LE8—2B 22
Chapel La. LE9—4A 24
Chapel St. LE2—5D 16
Chapel St. LE7—5A 28
Chapel St. LE8—3D 20
Chapel St. LE9—1F 19
Chapman St. LE11—2G 27
Chappell Clo. LE4—1F 5
Charlecote Av. LE3—2A 14
Charles Dri. LE7—2E 3
Charles St. LE1—3G 9
Charles St. LE11—2F 27
Charles Way. LE2—6F 17
Charley Dri. LE11—4D 26
Charlotte Ct. LE8—4C 20
Charnor Rd. LE3—2A 8
Charnwood. LE6—1B 6
Charnwood Av. LE4—1G 5
Charnwood Av. LE8—4A 20
Charnwood Clo. LE3—5E 7
Charnwood Dri. LE3—6F 7
Charnwood Dri. LE7—4H 11
Charnwood Precinct. LE11 —3F 27
Charnwood Rd. LE7—2D 2
Charnwood Rd. LE11—5F 27
Charnwood St. LE5—3A 10
Charnwood Wlk. LE5—3A 10
Charteris Clo. LE11—1C 26
Charter St. LE1—2G 9
Chartley Rd. LE3—6D 8
Chartwell Dri. LE8—1H 21
Chartwell Trading Est. LE8 —1G 21
Chase, The. LE3—4A 14
Chase, The. LE7—1D 28
Chater Clo. LE5—2G 11
Chatham St. LE1—4G 9
Chatsworth Av. LE8—3F 21
Chatsworth Dri. LE7—5A 28
Chatsworth Rd. LE11—2C 26
Chatsworth St. LE2—4A 10
Chatteris Av. LE5—6G 11
Chaucer St. LE2—6A 10
Chaucer St. LE9—3E 19
Cheapside. LE1—4F 9
Checketts Clo. LE4—5D 4
Checketts Rd. LE4—5D 4
Checkland Rd. LE4—1G 5
Cheddar Rd. LE8—1B 22
Chelker Way. LE11—4B 26
Chellaston Rd. LE8—1A 22
Cheltenham Rd. LE4—6H 3
Cheney End. LE9—4C 18
Chepstow Rd. LE2—6A 10
Cheriton Rd. LE2—5E 15
Cherry Dri. LE7—6B 28
Cherryleas Dri. LE3—5D 8
Cherry Rd. LE8—5C 20
Cherry St. LE8—2H 21
Cherry Tree Av. LE3—6D 6
Cherrytree Clo. LE7—3D 2
Cherry Tree Clo. LE8—1G 25
Cherry Tree Ct. LE3—6D 6
Cherry Tree Gro. LE9—1F 19
Cheshire Dri. LE8—1G 21
Cheshire Gdns. LE2—4E 15
Cheshire Rd. LE2—4E 15
Chester Clo. LE1—3H 9
Chester Clo. LE8—5D 20
Chester Clo. LE11—3E 27
Chesterfield Rd. LE5—5B 10
Chester Rd. LE8—5D 20
Chesterton Ct. LE9—2E 19
Chestnut Av. LE2—5D 16
Chestnut Av. LE5—1F 11
Chestnut Clo. LE7—4D 28 (Queniborough)
Chestnut Clo. LE7—6A 28 (Syston)
Chestnut Clo. LE9—5F 19
Chestnut Rd. LE3—1G 7
Chestnuts, The. LE8—1H 25
Chestnut St. LE11—3E 27
Chestnut Way. LE7—2D 28
Chettle Rd. LE3—2B 8
Chevin Av. LE3—4G 7
Chichester Clo. LE11—6C 26
Chilcombe Clo. LE4—4B 4
Chilcombe Wlk. LE4—5B 4
Chiltern Av. LE9—3B 24
Chiltern Grn. LE2—4G 15
Chislehurst Av. LE3—3A 14
Chiswick Dri. LE11—2B 26
Chiswick Rd. LE2—2F 15
Chorley Wood Rd. LE5—5G 11
Chrisett Clo. LE5—3E 11
Christie Dri. LE11—1C 26
Christopher Clo. LE8—2G 25
Christopher Dri. LE4—4H 5
Christow St. LE1—3H 9
Church Av. LE3—4D 8
Church Ga. LE1—3F 9
Church Ga. LE11—2F & 2G 27
Church Hill. LE4—2D 4
Church Hill. LE7—2H 11
Church Hill Rd. LE4—1G 5
Churchill Clo. LE2—5D 16
Churchill Dri. LE3—5F 7
Churchill St. LE2—5H 9
Church La. LE2—3H 15 (Knighton)
Church La. LE2—2G 17 (Stoughton)
Church La. LE4—1F 5
Church La. LE6—1B 6
Church La. LE7—2D 2
Church La. LE8—4A 20
Church La. LE9—4G 19
Church Nook. LE8—1B 22
Church Rd. LE2—4D 14
Church Rd. LE3—1F 7
Church Rd. LE4—5C 4
Church Rd. LE5—1E 17
Church Rd. LE9—4C 6
Church St. LE1—4G 9
Church St. LE2—5D 16
Church St. LE4—2F 5
Church St. LE8—4D 20 (Blaby)
Church St. LE8—2H 25 (Countesthorpe)
Church St. LE9—2A 18
Church View. LE9—4G 19
Church Wlk. LE4—5C 4
Church Wlk. LE8—4C 20
Churchward Av. LE4—4H 3
Circle, The. LE5—5C 10
Clarefield Rd. LE3—4C 8
Claremont St. LE4—5D 4
Clarence Rd. LE9—2H 19
Clarence St. LE1—3G 9
Clarence St. LE11—2G 27
Clarendon Pk. Rd. LE2—2H 15
Clarendon St. LE2—5F 9
Clarke Gro. LE4—3C 4
Clarkes Rd. LE8—2H 21
Clarke St. LE4—5D 4
Clawson Clo. LE11—1C 26
Claybrooke Av. LE3—3B 14
Claydon Rd. LE5—2C 10
Claymill Rd. LE4—4G 5
Clayton Dri. LE4—2G 5
Cleeve Mt. LE11—2B 26
Clement Av. LE4—5D 4
Clevedon Cres. LE4—1B 10
Cleveland Rd. LE8—1B 22
Cleveland Rd. LE11—6E 27
Cleveleys Av. LE3—3B 14
Cliff Av. LE11—1E 27
Cliffe Rd. LE4—2B 4
Clifford Rd. LE11—2E 27
Clifford St. LE3—4E 9
Clifford St. LE8—3F 21
Cliffwood Av. LE4—1C 4
Clifton Dri. LE8—3G 21
Clifton Rd. LE2—3F 15
Clipper Rd. LE4—5G 5
Clipstone Clo. LE8—2C 22
Clipstone Ho. LE2—4H 9
Close, The. LE6—1B 6
Close, The. LE7—2D 2
Close, The. LE8—3C 20
Clovelly Rd. LE3—1H 7
Clovelly Rd. LE5—5D 10
Clover Wlk. LE7—2D 28
Clowbridge Dri. LE11—4B 26
Clumber Clo. LE7—4B 28
Clumber Rd. LE5—4B 10
Clyde St. LE1—3G 9
Coalbourn Clo. LE4—4B 4
Coatbridge Av. LE4—4F 5
Coates Av. LE3—2B 8
Cobden St. LE1—2H 9
Cobden St. LE11—3G 27
Coe Av. LE11—2B 26
Cokayne Rd. LE3—4H 7
Colbert Dri. LE3—4B 14
Colby Dri. LE4—3H 5
Colby Rd. LE4—3G 5
Colchester Rd. LE5—3E 11
Colebrook Clo. LE5—6C 10
Colebrook Wlk. LE5—6C 10
Coleman Rd. LE5—3C 10 to 5E 11
Coleridge Dri. LE9—2E 19
Coles Clo. LE4—3F 5
Colgrove Rd. LE11—4E 27
Colindale Av. LE4—1C 4
Collaton Rd. LE8—2A 22
College Av. LE2—5H 9
College Hall. LE2—3A 16
College Rd. LE7—6B 28
College Rd. LE8—4B 20
College St. LE2—5H 9
Collett Rd. LE4—4H 3
Collingham Rd. LE3—1D 14
Collin Pl. LE4—6E 5
Colne Clo. LE2—5G 17
Colsterdale Clo. LE4—3A 4
Coltbeck Av. LE9—4E 19
Colthurst Way. LE5—4H 11
Colton St. LE1—4G 9
Columbia Clo. LE9—1E 19
Columbine Clo. LE3—1H 13
Colwell Rd. LE3—2E 9
Combe Clo. LE3—2D 8
Comet Clo. LE3—2C 8
Commercial Sq. LE2—1F 15
Common, The. LE5—6E 11
Compass Rd. LE5—3F 11
Compton Dri. LE9—4C 18
Compton Rd. LE3—1D 14
Conaglen Rd. LE2—5C 14
Conduit St. LE2—5H 9
Coneries, The. LE11—2G 27
Conery La. LE9—1F 19
Conifer Clo. LE2—5A 10
Coninsby Clo. LE3—1C 14
Coniston Av. LE2—6F 9
Coniston Cres. LE11—5C 26
Coniston Way. LE9—6B 24
Connaught St. LE2—5H 9
Constable Av. LE4—2H 9
Constance Rd. LE5—5B 10
Constitution Hill. LE1—4H 9
Conway Clo. LE11—2B 26
Conway Rd. LE2—6A 10
Cooden Av. LE3—5C 8
Cooks La. LE8—4B 22
Cookson Pl. LE11—1B 26
Cooks Wlk. LE3—2G 7
Coombe Pl. LE2—1E 23
Coombe Rise. LE2—1F 23
Co-operation St. LE9—1F 19
Cooper Clo. LE2—5D 14 (in two parts)
Cooper Clo. LE9—4C 18
Cooper Ct. LE11—4H 27
Cooper's Nook. LE7—2C 28
Cooper St. LE4—1G 9
Copdale Rd. LE5—4B 10
Copeland Av. LE3—1B 8
Copeland Rd. LE4—2C 4
Copinger Rd. LE2—3F 15
Coplow Av. LE5—1C 16
Coplow Cres. LE7—6A 28
Coppice Hall. LE2—3D 16
Coppice, The. LE8—2G 25
Coppice, The. LE9—4F 19
Copse Clo. LE2—4F 17
Copt Oak Rd. LE9—3E 19
Corah St. LE3—4E 9
Coral St. LE4—6C 4
Corbet Clo. LE4—5G 3
Cordell Rd. LE11—1C 26
Cordery Rd. LE5—6E 11
Corfield Rise. LE3—6A 8
Cork La. LE2—2C 20
Cork St. LE5—5A 10
Cornwallis Av. LE4—6G 3
Cornwall Rd. LE4—1E 9
Cornwall Rd. LE8—2G 21
Cornwall St. LE9—2F 19
Coronation Av. LE8—2H 21
Corporation Rd. LE4—6B 4
Corshaw Wlk. LE5—2B 10
Cort Cres. LE3—5A 8 to 1B 14
Cosby Rd. LE8—2E 25
Cosby Rd. LE9—6G 19
Cossington La. LE7—2A 28
Cossington St. LE4—1H 9
Cothelstone Av. LE11—2B 26
Cotley Rd. LE4—3H 3
Cotswold Av. LE9—3B 24
Cotswold Clo. LE11—3C 26
Cotswold Grn. LE4—3H 3
Cottage Clo. LE6—1B 6
Cottage Rd. LE8—3B 22
Cottage Row. LE3—3C 14
Cottagers Clo. LE2—6F 15
Cottesbrooke Clo. LE8—2B 22
Cottesmore Av. LE2—6G 17
Cottesmore Dri. LE11—6E 27
Cottesmore Rd. LE5—2B 10
Cotton Clo. LE4—3F 5
Cotton Way. LE11—1D 26
Countesthorpe Rd. LE8—6F to 3F 21
Countesthorpe Rd. LE9 & LE8 —3A to 2D 24
Countryman's Way. LE7—1D 28
Court Clo. LE9—4C 6
Courtenay Rd. LE3—1D 8
Court Rd. LE2—2C 20
Court Rd. LE7—5H 11
Coventry Rd. LE9—6B 24 (Croft)
Coventry Rd. LE9—6D 18 to 5F 19 (Narborough)
Coverack Wlk. LE5—5D 10
Coverdale Rd. LE8—3C 22
Covert Clo. LE2—4F 17
Covert La. LE7—2H 11
Covert, The. LE7—1D 28
Covett Way. LE3—4H 7
Cowdall Rd. LE3—6H 7
Cowdray Clo. LE11—5F 27
Cowley Way. LE5—3H 11
Crabtree Corner. LE2—6G 15
Cradock Rd. LE2—1H 15
Cradock St. LE5—3H 9
Cradock St. LE11—2G 27
Crafton St. E. LE1—3H 9
Crafton St. W. LE1—3G 9
Craig Gdns. LE3—3H 7
Craighill Rd. LE2—2H 15
Craighill Wlk. LE2—3H 15
Cranberry Clo. LE3—1H 13
Cranborne Gdns. LE2—3E 17
Cranbrook Rd. LE7—3H 11
Crane Ley Rd. LE6—2B 2
Crane St. LE1—3F 9
Cranfield Rd. LE2—5E 15
Cranmer Clo. LE8—5B 20
Cranmer Dri. LE7—5A 28
Cranmer St. LE3—5E 9
Cranstone Cres. LE3—3G 7
Crantock Clo. LE5—6F 11
Cranwell Clo. LE5—1E 17
Craven Clo. LE11—6E 27
Craven St. LE1—3F 9
Crayburn Ho. LE3—2B 8
Crayford Way. LE5—1G 11
Creaton Rd. LE8—2C 22
Crediton Clo. LE8—4B 22
Crescent St. LE1—5G 9
Crescent, The. LE8—5C 20 (Blaby)
Crescent, The. LE8—6A 16 (Wigston)
Cressida Pl. LE3—1A 14
Crestway, The. LE8—4B 20
Crete Av. LE8—2E 21
Critchlow Rd. LE9—4C 18
Croft Av. LE2—4D 14
Croft Dri. LE8—6H 15
Croft Hill Rd. LE9—5B 18
Croft Rd. LE9—2A 24 (Cosby)
Croft Rd. LE9—3A 18 (Thurlaston)
Croft, The. LE9—4C 6
Cromarty Clo. LE4—5F 5
Cromer St. LE2—6A 10
Cromford Av. LE8—3G 21
Cromford Rd. LE9—1B 24
Cromford St. LE2—4A 10
Cromwell Rd. LE2—2F 15
Croome Clo. LE11—5G 27
Cropston Av. LE11—4A 26
Cropston Rd. LE7—2E 3
Cropthorne Av. LE5—4C 10
Cross Hedge Clo. LE4—4H 3
Cross Hill La. LE11—6E & 6F 27
Cross Keys Grn. LE5—3G 11
Crossley St. LE3—1G 7
Cross Rd. LE2—1A 16
Cross St. LE2—4D 16
Cross St. LE4—1G 9
Cross St. LE7—5A 28
Cross St. LE8—4C 20 (Blaby)
Cross St. LE8—2B 22 (Wigston)
Cross St. LE9—1F 19
Cross St. LE11—2G 27
Cross, The. LE9—1F 19
Cross Wlk. LE5—4D 10
Crossways, The. LE4—1D 4
Crossway, The. LE2—4F 15
Crossway, The. LE3—2B 14
Crowan Dri. LE8—3A 22
Crowhurst Dri. LE3—3A 14
Crow La. LE3—6E 9
Crown Hills Av. LE5—4C 10
Crown Hills Rise. LE5—5C 10
Croyde Clo. LE5—5D 10
Croyland Grn. LE5—3H 11
Cufflin Clo. LE6—2C 6
Cuffling Clo. LE3—4H 7
Cuffling Dri. LE3—4G 7
Culham Av. LE5—1B 10
Culver Rd. LE3—2D 8
Culworth Dri. LE8—2C 22
Cumberland Rd. LE8—1F 21
Cumberland Rd. LE11—2E 27
Cumberland St. LE1—3F 9
Cumberwell Dri. LE9—3G 19
Curlew Wlk. LE5—3A 10
Curteys Clo. LE3—2C 14
Curtis Clo. LE8—4B 20
Curzon Av. LE4—2C 4
Curzon Av. LE8—3G 21
Curzon Rd. LE2—4E 15
Curzon St. LE1—2H 9
Curzon St. LE11—3F 27
Cutters Clo. LE9—5F 19
Cyprus Rd. LE2—4E 15
Cyril St. LE3—3C 14

Dakyn Rd. LE5—4G 11
Dalby Dri. LE6—5A 2
Dalby Rd. LE7—2D 2
Dale Acre. LE8—2H 25
Dale Av. LE8—6H 15
Dale St. LE2—4A 10
Dalkeith Rd. LE4—4E 5
Dalley Clo. LE7—6B 28
Dane Hill. LE6—1B 6
Danehurst Av. LE3—3C 8
Daneshill Rd. LE3—4D 8
Dannett St. LE3—4E 9
Dannett Wlk. LE3—4E 9
Danvers Rd. LE3—6D 8
Darenth Dri. LE4—5F 3
Darker St. LE1—3F 9
Darley Av. LE8—3G 21
Darley Rd. LE8—4B 20
Darley St. LE2—4A 10
Darlington Rd. LE3—1C 8
Dart Clo. LE2—5F 17
Dartford Rd. LE2—2E 15
Darwen Clo. LE3—1C 8
Dashwood Rd. LE2—6A 10
Davenport Av. LE2—5D 16
Davenport Rd. LE5—4E 11
Davenport Rd. LE8—3A 22
Davett Clo. LE5—3E 11
David Av. LE4—3A 4
Davison Clo. LE5—3D 10
Dawlish Clo. LE5—5G 11
Day St. LE4—5C 4
Deacon St. LE2—5F 9
Dead La. LE11—2F 27
Deancourt Rd. LE2—5H 15
Deane St. LE11—2D 26
Dean Rd. LE4—1A 10
Deansburn Ho. LE3—2B 8
Deanside Dri. LE11—1D 26
Deepdale. LE5—3D 10
Deighton Way. LE11—1C 26
Delaware Rd. LE5—6G 11
De Montfort Pl. LE1—5H 9
De Montfort Sq. LE1—5G 9
De Montfort St. LE1—6G 9
Denacre Av. LE8—3G 21
Denegate Av. LE4—1B 4
Denis Clo. LE3—4C 8
Denman La. LE9—4C 18
Denmark Rd. LE2—3F 15
Denmead Av. LE8—1A 22
Denton St. LE3—4C 8
Denton Wlk. LE8—2C 22
Derby Rd. LE11—1C 26 to 2F 27
Derby Sq. LE11—3F 27
Derry Wlk. LE4—4A 4
Dersingham Rd. LE4—6A 4
Derwent Dri. LE11—5C 26 (in two parts)
Derwent St. LE2—4A 10
Derwent Wlk. LE2—5F 17
Desford La. LE9 & LE6—4B to 2B 6
Desford Rd. LE9—2A 12 to 6E 13 (Enderby)
Desford Rd. LE9—4C 6 (Kirby Muxloe)
Desford Rd. LE9—4F 19 (Narborough)
Desford Rd. LE9—1A 18 (Thurlaston)
Devana Rd. LE2—6A 10
Devonshire Av. LE8—3G 21
Devonshire Rd. LE4—1E 9
Devonshire Sq. LE11—3F 27
Devonshire St. LE1—3F 9
Devonshire Wlk. LE2—1F 23
Devon Way. LE5—4D 10
Dickens Ct. LE3—5B 8
Dicken, The. LE8—5A 20
Didsbury St. LE3—6A 8
Digby Clo. LE3—6C 8
Digby Ho. LE2—3C 16
Dillon Rise. LE3—1A 8
Dillon Rd. LE3—1A 8
Dillon Way. LE3—1B 8
Dimmingsdale Clo. LE7—1E 3
Dingley Av. LE4—1A 10
Dingley Link. LE8—1C 22
Diseworth St. LE2—4A 10
Disraeli St. LE2—4D 14
Ditchling Av. LE3—3C 8
Dixon Dri. LE2—6A 10
Dobney Av. LE7—3C 28
Dog & Gun La. LE8—6A 20
Dominion Rd. LE3—2G 7
Donaldson Rd. LE4—1G 9
Doncaster Rd. LE4—1H 9
Donnett Clo. LE5—3E 11
Donnington St. LE2—4A 10
Dorchester Clo. LE8—6D 20 (Blaby)
Dorchester Clo. LE8—4A 22 (Wigston)
Dorchester Rd. LE3—5C 8
Dore Rd. LE5—5A 10
Dorfold Wlk. LE4—1B 10
Dorothy Av. LE2—1C 20
Dorothy Av. LE4—2F 5
Dorothy Rd. LE5—4B 10
Dorset Av. LE3—1G 7
Dorset Av. LE8—1F 21
Dorset St. LE4—1H 9
Dovecote La. LE9—5A 24
Dovedale Av. LE8—4C 20
Dovedale Ct. LE2—2B 16
Dovedale Rd. LE2—2B 16
Dovedale Rd. LE4—2G 5
Dove Rise. LE2—5F 17
Dover St. LE1—5G 9
Downham Av. LE4—6B 4
Downing Dri. LE5—6F 11
Down St. LE4—6D 4

Doyle Clo. LE11—1C 26
Draper St. LE2—6A 10
Drayton Rd. LE3—3H 7
Drinkstone Rd. LE5—5B 10
Drive, The. LE4—2C 4
Drive, The. LE7—1H 11
Drive, The. LE8—2F 25
Dronfield St. LE5—5A 10
Drumcliff Rd. LE5—4H 11
Drummond Rd. LE4—5C 4
Drummmond Rd. LE9—1E 19
Drury La. LE2—4C 16
Dryden St. LE1—3G 9
Dudleston Clo. LE5—4E 11
Dudley Av. LE5—3F 11
Dudley Clo. LE5—3F 11
Duffield Av. LE8—6H 15
Duffield St. LE2—4A 10
Dukes Clo. LE8—1H 21
Dukes Dri. LE2—1A 16
Duke St. LE1—5G 9
Duke St. LE11—2G 27
Dulverton Clo. LE8—4B 22
Dulverton Clo. LE11—6C 26
Dulverton Rd. LE3—5D 8
Dumbleton Av. LE3—1D 14
Dunbar Rd. LE4—6F 5
Dunblane Av. LE4—4F 5
Duncan Av. LE9—4C 18
Duncan Rd. LE2—3E 15
Duncan Way. LE11—1B 26
Dundee Rd. LE8—6C 20
Dundonald Rd. LE4—1G 9
Dunholme Av. LE11—2B 26
Dunholme Rd. LE4—1B 10
Dunire Clo. LE4—5H 3
Dunkirk St. LE1—5G 9
Dunlin Rd. LE5—3A 10
Duns La. LE3—4E 9
Dunstall Av. LE3—1H 13
Dunster St. LE3—5C 8
Dunsville Wlk. LE4—5F 5
Dunton St. LE3—3E 9
Dunton St. LE8—3G 21
Dupont Clo. LE3—3H 7
Dupont Gdns. LE3—3G 7
Durham Dri. LE8—1G 21
Durham Rd. LE11—1D 26
Durnford Rd. LE8—4A 22
Durston Clo. LE5—5G 11
Duxbury Rd. LE5—3B 10
Dysart Way. LE1—2G 9

Ealing Rd. LE2—2F 15
Eamont Clo. LE2—1E 21
Eamont Grn. LE2—1E 21
Earl Howe St. LE2—5H 9
Earl Howe Ter. LE3—5E 9
Earl Russell St. LE2—4D 14
Earl Smith Clo. LE8—5B 20
Earl St. LE1—3G 9
Earl's Way. LE4—1H 5
Earlswood Rd. LE5—6G 11
East Av. LE2—1A 16
East Av. LE7—5B 28
East Av. LE8—4B 20
E. Bond St. LE1—3F 9
Eastcourt Rd. LE2—4A 16
Eastern Boulevd. LE2—6E 9
Eastfield Rd. LE3—4C 8
Eastfield Rd. LE4—1H 5
E. Gates. LE1—4F 9
Eastleigh Rd. LE3—6D 8
Eastmere Rd. LE8—1D 22
E. Park Rd. LE5—5A 10
East Rd. LE4—4C 4
East St. LE1—5G 9
East St. LE2—5D 16
East Wlk. LE6—1B 6
Eastway Rd. LE8—6B 16
Eastwood Rd. LE2—5E 15
Ebchester Clo. LE2—1D 20
Ebchester Rd. LE2—1D 20
Edale Clo. LE3—6A 8
Eddystone Rd. LE5—3H 11
Edelin Rd. LE11—5F 27
Eden Clo. LE2—4F 17
Eden Clo. LE11—1C 26
Edenhall Clo. LE4—5F 5
Edenhurst Av. LE3—3B 14
Eden Rd. LE2—4F 17
Edensor St. LE4—5E 5
Eden Way. LE2—2E 21
Edgecote Ct. LE5—2B 10
Edgehill Rd. LE4—6F 5
Edgeley Rd. LE8—1H 25
Edith Av. LE3—4B 14
Edmonton Rd. LE1—3G 9
Edward Av. LE3—3A 14
Edward Clo. LE2—6F 17
Edward Rd. LE2—1H 15
Edward St. LE5—3A 10
Edward St. LE7—2D 2
Edward St. LE11—2E 27
Egerton Av. LE4—6B 4
Eggington Ct. LE11—4D 26
Egginton St. LE5—5A 10
Eileen Av. LE4—6B 4
Elbow La. LE1—3F 9
Eldon St. LE1—3G 9
Elgin Av. LE3—2B 8
Elizabeth Ct. LE8—2A 22
Elizabeth Cres. LE8—1H 21
Elizabeth Dri. LE2—6F 17
Elizabeth Dri. LE4—1G 5
Elizabeth Gdns. LE8—5A 20
Elizabeth Ho. LE3—2B 8
Elizabeth St. LE5—4C 10
Ellaby Rd. LE11—1C 26
Elland Rd. LE3—4F 7
Ellesmere Pl. LE3—1C 14
Ellesmere Rd. LE3—1C 14
Elliott Dri. LE3—6F 7
Elliott Dri. LE4—2H 5
Elliott Rd. LE4—4A 4
Ellis Av. LE4—6C 4
Ellis Clo. LE3—2G 7
Ellis Dri. LE3—6D 6
Ellis St. LE7—2D 2
Ellys St. LE3—4E 9
Elmcroft Av. LE5—3E 11
Elmdale St. LE4—5C 4
Elmfield Av. LE2—6A 10
Elmfield Av. LE4—1B 4
Elms Clo. LE2—6E 17
Elms Gro. LE11—3G 27
Elmsleigh Av. LE2—2B 16
Elms Rd. LE2—2A 16
Elms Rd. Houses. LE2—3B 16
Elms, The. LE8—4C 20
(Blaby)
Elms, The. LE8—1H 25
(Countesthorpe)
Elmsthorpe Rise. LE3—6C 8
Elm Tree Av. LE3—2F 7
Elm Tree Rd. LE9—3A 24
Elmwood Row. LE2—6G 15
Elsadene Av. LE4—5D 4
Elsalene Dri. LE6—1A 2
Elsham Clo. LE3—4H 7
Elston Fields. LE2—5F 15
Elstree Av. LE5—1G 11
Elsworthy Wlk. LE3—4H 7
Elwin Av. LE8—6B 16
Emberton Clo. LE8—2C 22
Emburn Ho. LE3—2B 8
Emerson Clo. LE4—5G 3
Empire Rd. LE3—3D 8
Empress Rd. LE11—3G 27
Enderby Rd. LE8—3A to 4C 20
Enderby Rd. LE9—1A 18
Englefield Rd. LE5—5G 11
Ensbury Gdns. LE5—6E 11
Epinal Way. LE11—3D 26
Epping Way. LE2—1D 20
Epsom Rd. LE4—6D 4
Equity Rd. LE3—6E 9
Equity Rd. LE9—2F 19
Erdyngton Rd. LE3—5A 8
Eric Wood Building. LE2—5F 9
Erith Rd. LE2—2E 15
Erskine St. LE1—3G 9
Eskdale Ho. LE2—1D 20
Eskdale Rd. LE4—5H 3
Essex Lodge. LE11—3D 26
Essex Rd. LE4—6G 5
Essex Rd. LE8—1G 21
Estoril Av. LE8—1C 22
Ethel Rd. LE5—5B 10 to 5E 11
Eton Clo. LE2—3H 15
Eunice Av. LE9—4C 18
Euston St. LE2—2G 15
Evelyn Dri. LE3—1D 14
Evelyn Rd. LE3—1A 14
Everest Ct. LE1—3H 9
Everett Clo. LE4—2H 5
Every St. LE1—4G 9
Evesham Rd. LE3—1D 14
Evington Clo. LE5—6B 10
Evington Dri. LE5—6B 10
Evington Footpath. LE2—6H 9
Evington La. LE5—6B 10 to 1E 17
Evington Parks Rd. LE2—6B 10
Evington Pl. LE2—5A 10
Evington Rd. LE2—5H 9
Evington St. LE2—5H 9
Evington Valley Rd. LE5—6B 10
Exchange, The. LE2—1E 21
Exeter Rd. LE8—1H 21
Exmoor Av. LE4—1E 9
Exmoor Clo. LE8—3B 22
Exmoor Clo. LE11—6C 26
Exton Rd. LE5—2C 10
Eye Brook Clo. LE11—4A 26
Eynsford Clo. LE2—3C 16

Factory St. LE11—3G 27
Fairbourne Rd. LE3—2B 14
Fairburn Ho. LE3—2B 8
Fairefield Cres. LE3—6D 2
Faire Rd. LE3—6D 2
Fairestone Av. LE3—2G 7
Fairfax Clo. LE4—6G 5
Fairfax Rd. LE4—6F 5
Fairfax St. LE2—5F 9
Fairfield Rd. LE2—5E 17
Fairfield St. LE5—4A 10
Fairfield St. LE8—3G 21
Fairford Av. LE5—6E 11
Fairholme Rd. LE2—5H 15
Fairisle Way. LE8—2H 25
Fairmount Dri. LE11—4D 26
Fairstone Hill. LE2—6E 17
Fairview Av. LE8—5A 20
Fairway, The. LE2—5G 15
(Aylestone)
Fairway, The. LE2—2D 16
(Oadby)
Fairway, The. LE8—5C 20
Fairway, The. LE9—5D 6
Falconer Cres. LE3—2H 7
Falcon Rd. LE7—3C 2
Faldo Clo. LE4—3F 5
Falkner Ct. LE11—4D 26
Fallowfield Rd. LE5—5G 11
Falmouth Dri. LE8—3A 22
Falmouth Rd. LE5—5D 10
Faraday Hall. LE11—4C 26
Farleigh Av. LE8—1A 22
Farley Rd. LE2—3B 16
Farm Clo. LE4—2D 4
Farm Clo., The. LE2—6F 15
Farmway. LE3—4A 14
Farndale. LE8—2C 22
Farndale Dri. LE11—6E 27
Farnham Rd. LE11—6F 27
Farnham St. LE5—3A 10
Farnworth Clo. LE4—5F 5
Farrier La. LE4—4G 3
Farrier's Way. LE7—2D 28
Farringdon St. LE5—2A 10
Farr Wood Clo. LE6—2A 2
Farthingdale Clo. LE9—2B 24
Fastnet Rd. LE5—2H 11
(in two parts)
Fayrhurst Rd. LE2—5F 15
Fearon St. LE11—2E 27
Featherby Dri. LE2—1C 20
Featherstone Dri. LE2—2D 20
Federation St. LE9—2F 19
Felley Way. LE3—1D 8
Felstead Rd. LE4—4A 4
Fennel St. LE11—2F 27
Fenton Clo. LE2—1E 23
Fermain Clo. LE5—5G 11
Fern Bank. LE5—3A 10
Fern Cres. LE6—2A 2
Ferndale Dri. LE6—1C 6
Ferndale Rd. LE2—5H 15
Ferndale Rd. LE4—2G 5
Fernhurst Rd. LE3—3A 14
Fernie Clo. LE2—6F 17
Fernie Rd. LE5—3B 10
Fernleys Clo. LE4—5G 3
Fern Rise. LE5—1F 11
Ferrers Rise. LE6—2B 2
Ferrers St. LE2—5G 15
Festival Av. LE4—2F 5
Festival Dri. LE11—1E 27
Field Ct. Rd. LE6—5A 2
Fieldfare Wlk. LE5—3A 10
Fieldgate Cres. LE4—1B 4
Field Ho. LE11—3D 26
Fieldhouse Rd. LE4—5D 4
Fieldhurst Av. LE3—3A 14
Fielding Rd. LE4—1B 4
Filbert St. LE2—6F 9
Filbert St. E. LE2—6F 9
Finch Clo. LE3—4A 8
Fineshade Av. LE3—1D 8
Finsbury Av. LE11—4G 27
Finsbury Rd. LE4—1A 10
Finson Clo. LE8—1B 22
Fiona Dri. LE7—4H 11
Firfield Av. LE4—1C 4
Fir Tree Av. LE8—1G 25
Fir Tree Clo. LE8—6A 16
Firtree La. LE6—2A 2
Firtree Wlk. LE6—2B 2
Fishponds Clo. LE3—1F 7
Fishpools. LE3—4A 14
Fitzwilliam Clo. LE2—6G 17
Flamborough Rd. LE5—3F 11
Flatholme Rd. LE5—1H 11
Flatten Way. LE7—4A 28
Flaxfield Clo. LE6—3B 2
Flax Rd. LE4—6D 4
Fleet St. LE1—3G 9
Fleetwood Rd. LE2—2H 15
Fleming Clo. LE11—1C 26
Fletcher's Way. LE7—2C 28
(in two parts)
Flora St. LE3—4D 8
Florence Av. LE8—3G 21
Florence Rd. LE5—3A 10
Florence St. LE2—4E 15
Floyd Clo. LE4—3G 5
Fludes La. LE2—6F 17
Folville Rise. LE3—1C 14
Fontwell Dri. LE2—6C 14
Forbes Clo. LE3—3G 7
Ford Clo. LE2—1D 20
Ford Rise. LE2—1D 20
Ford, The. LE2—3D 20
Forest Av. LE4—1F 5
Forest Clo. LE6—2A 2
Forest Ct. LE11—4F 27
Forest Dri. LE7—4H 11
Forest Dri. LE9—5D 6
Forester's Row. LE7—2D 28
Forest Ga. LE7—2C 2
Forest Rise. LE2—4F 17
Forest Rise. LE3—6D 6
Forest Rise. LE6—2A 2
Forest Rd. LE5—2A 10
Forest Rd. LE9—6D 12 to 4F 19
(Enderby)
Forest Rd. LE9—4C to 1C 18
(Huncote)
Forest Rd. LE11—5D 26 to 4F 27
Forrester Clo. LE9—2B 24
Forryan Clo. LE9—3B 24
Fosse La. LE3—2D 8
Fosse Rd. Central. LE3—4D 8
Fosse Rd. N. LE3—3D 8
(in two parts)
Fosse Rd. S. LE3—1C 14 to 5D 8
Fosse Way. LE7—4A 28
Foston Rd. LE8—1H 25
Foundry La. LE1—2G 9
Foundry La. LE7—6A 28
Foundry Sq. LE1—2G 9
Fountains Av. LE2—1E 21
Fowler Clo. LE4—4H 3
Foxcroft Clo. LE3—3D 14
Foxglove Clo. LE7—1D 28
Foxhill Dri. LE2—1B 20
Fox Hollow. LE7—1D 28
Foxhunter Dri. LE2—5C 16
Fox La. LE1—4G 9
Fox La. LE9—4C 6
Foxon St. LE3—5E 9
Fox St. LE1—4G 9
Framland Ho. LE2—4H 9
Frampton Av. LE3—5C 8
Franche Rd. LE3—4D 8
Francis Av. LE3—3B 14
Francis St. LE2—1B 16
Franklyn Rd. LE2—5C 14
Frankson Av. LE3—2B 14
Fraser Clo. LE1—3G 9
Frederick Rd. LE5—3A 10
Frederick St. LE8—1B 22
Frederick St. LE11—3F 27
Fredscott Clo. LE5—2G 11
Freeboard Rd. LE3—3A 14
Freehold Rd. LE4—3C 4
Freehold St. LE1—3H 9
Freehold St. LE11—2G 27
Free La. LE1—4G 9
Freeman Rd. N. LE5—3C 10
Freeman's Cotts. LE2—1G 15
Freeman's Way. LE7—1D 28
Freemantle Rd. LE2—2B 16
Freemen's Comn. Rd. LE2—1F 15
Freemen's Holt. LE2—4D 14
Freer Clo. LE8—4C 20
Freeschool La. LE1—4F 9
French Rd. LE5—3B 10
Frensham Clo. LE2—1D 22
Freshwater Clo. LE8—4A 22
Frewin St. LE5—2B 10
Friar La. LE1—4F 9
Friars Causeway. LE1—4F 9
Frichley Clo. LE9—5C 18
Friday St. LE1—3F 9
Frinton Av. LE5—5F 11
Frisby Rd. LE5—2A 10
Frith Clo. LE3—2G 7
Frog Island. LE3—2E 9
Frolesworth Rd. LE3—3H 7
Frolesworth Way. LE3—3H 7
Frome Av. LE2—4G 17
Front St. LE4—2D 4
Fulbeck Av. LE5—5F 11
Fullhurst Av. LE3—6C 8
Fulmar Rd. LE7—3D 2

Gables Hall, The. LE2—3D 16
Gaddesby Av. LE3—6D 8
Gainsborough Rd. LE2—2H 15
Galaxy Wlk. LE2—4A 10
Galby St. LE5—2A 10
Gallards Hill. LE3—6H 7 to 5A 8
Gallico Clo. LE11—1C 26
Gallimore Clo. LE3—6D 2
Gallowtree Ga. LE1—4G 9
Galsworthy Ct. LE3—5B 8
Galway Rd. LE4—3A 4
Gamel Rd. LE5—4E 11
Gamel Wlk. LE5—4E 11
Garden Clo. LE2—5D 16
Gardenfield Rd. LE4—4G 5
Garden St. LE1—3G 9
Garden St. LE4—1F 5
Garden St. LE8—3G 21
Gardiner Clo. LE11—1C 26
Garendon Grn. LE11—3C & 3D 26
Garendon Rd. LE11—3C 26
Garendon St. LE2—4H 9
Garendon Way. LE11—2D 26
Garfield St. LE4—2G 9
Garfit Rd. LE9—4D 6
Garland Cres. LE3—2C 8
Garnett Cres. LE2—1D 20
Garsdale. LE8—2C 22
Garsington Wlk. LE5—3D 10
Garth Av. LE4—4A 4
Garton Rd. LE11—4F 27
Gartree Rd. LE2—2C 16 to 4H 17
Gaskell Wlk. LE3—5B 8
Gas La. LE8—3A 22
Gas St. LE1—2G 9
Gateway St. LE2—5F 9
Gaulby La. LE2—3F to 2H 17
Gaul St. LE3—5E 9
Gavin Dri. LE11—1C 26
Gayhurst Clo. LE3—3A 14
Gayhurst Clo. LE8—2C 22
Gayton Av. LE4—1A 10
Gedding Rd. LE5—5B 10
Geddington Clo. LE8—2B 22
Gedge Way. LE2—4F 15
Gees Lock Clo. LE2—6C 14
Gelert Av. LE5—4G 11
Georgeham Clo. LE8—3B 22
George St. LE1—3G 9
George St. LE7—2D 2
George St. LE9—1F 19
George St. LE11—2E 27
George Yd. LE11—3F 27
Gervas Rd. LE5—3F 11
Gibbon's Clo. LE4—1H 9
Gifford Clo. LE5—6E 11
Gilbert Clo. LE4—4F 5
Gilbert Murray Hall. LE2—3D 16
Gillam Butts. LE8—2G 25
Gillbank Dri. LE6—2B 6
Gilliver St. LE2—3H 15
Gillman Rd. LE3—2B 8
Gilmorton Av. LE2—6C 14
Gilmorton Clo. LE2—6C 14
Gimson Av. LE9—2B 24
Gimson Hall. LE1—5G 9
Gimson Rd. LE3—4C 8
Gipsy La. LE4 & LE5—6E 5 to 1D 10
Gipsy Rd. LE4—6D 4
Gisbourne Ct. LE5—1E 17
Glade, The. LE3—4A 14
Gladstone Av. LE11—2F 27
Gladstone St. LE1—3G 9
Gladstone St. LE7—2E 3
Gladstone St. LE8—1A 22
Gladstone St. LE11—2F 27
Glaisdale Clo. LE4—5H 3
Glaisdale Rd. LE8—3C 22
Glamorgan Av. LE8—2F 21
Glazebrook Rd. LE3—1B 8
Glazebrook Sq. LE3—1B 8
Glebe Clo. LE2—3C 16
Glebe Clo. LE8—1B 22
Glebe Dri. LE8—2G 25
Glebe Rd. LE2—3C 16
Glebe Rd. LE6—3B 2
Glebe Rd. LE7—4D 28
Glebe St. LE2—5H 9
Glebe St. LE11—1G 27
Glenbarr Av. LE4—2E 9
Glenborne Rd. LE2—6G 15
Glencoe Av. LE4—4E 5
Glendale Av. LE3—5B 2
Glendon St. LE4—1H 9
Glendower Clo. LE5—3E 11
Gleneagles Av. LE4—4F & 5F 5
Gleneagles Wlk. LE4—4E 5
Glenfield Cres. LE3—2G 7
Glenfield Frith Dri. LE3—1G 7
Glenfield La. LE9—3D 6
Glenfield Rd. LE3—3A to 4D 8
Glenfrith Rd. LE3—6F 3
Glengarry Way. LE3—2A 8
Glengate. LE8—3G 21
Glenhills Boulevd. LE2—6D 14 & 6E 15
Glenmore Rd. LE4—5F 5
Glen Pk. Av. LE3—6B 2
Glen Rise. LE2—1C 20
(Glen Parva)
Glen Rise. LE2—2H 23
(Oadby)
Glen Rd. LE2—6F 17
Glen Rd. LE8—5G 23
Glen St. LE4—6D 4
Glenville Av. LE2—2C 20
Glenville Av. LE3—6C 2
Glen Way. LE2—1F 23
Glenwood Clo. LE2—2B 16
Glossop St. LE5—6A 10
Gloucester Av. LE7—5B 28
Gloucester Cres. LE8—1F 21
Glovers Wlk. LE4—4H 3
Goddard's Clo. LE2—5D 16
Goddards Clo. LE4—6G 3
Godstow Wlk. LE5—4D 10
Godwin Av. LE8—2B 22
Goldhill. LE2—6G 15
Goldhill Rd. LE2—3B 16
Golf Course La. LE3—5G 7
Goodes Av. LE7—6A 28
Goode's La. LE7—6A 28
Gooding Av. LE3—5A to 6C 8
Gooding Clo. LE3—6C 8
Goodwood Cres. LE5—5E 11
Goodwood Rd. LE5—3E to 6E 11
Gopsall St. LE2—5H 9

Gordon Av. LE2—5H 9
Gordon Ho. LE2—4H 9
Gorseburn Ho. LE3—2A 8
Gorse Hill. LE7—3E 3
Gorse La. LE2—1G 23
Gorsty Clo. LE4—5G 3
Goscote Hall Rd. LE4—2C 4
Gosling St. LE2—5F 9
Gotham St. LE2—5H 9
Gough Rd. LE5—3B 10
Gower St. LE1—3G 9
Gracedieu Rd. LE11—3C 26
Grace Rd. LE2—3E 15
Grafton Dri. LE8—2D 22
Grafton Pl. LE1—3F 9
Grafton Rd. LE11—1D 26
Graham Rise. LE11—1C 26
Graham St. LE5—3H 9
Granby Av. LE5—3A 10
Granby Pl. LE1—4G 9
Granby Rd. LE2—3E 15
Granby St. LE1—4G 9
Granby St. LE11—3F 27
Grange Av. LE3—6F 7
Grange Clo. LE3—1F 7
Grange Clo. LE6—2C 6
Grange Dri. LE2—1D 20
Grange Dri. LE8—4A 20
Grange La. LE2—5F 9
Grange La. LE7—5H 11
Grange Rd. LE8—6A 16
Grange St. LE11—2E 27
Grangeway Rd. LE8—6A 16
Grantham Rd. LE5—2F 11
Grant Way. LE2—6F 15
Granville Av. LE2—4C 16
Granville Cres. LE8—6H 15
Granville Rd. LE1—6H 9
Granville Rd. LE8—6H 15
Granville St. LE11—3E 27
Grape St. LE1—3F 9
Grasmere Rd. LE8—1C 22
Grasmere Rd. LE11—6E 27
Grasmere St. LE2—5F 9
Grass Acres. LE3—4A 14
Grassholme Dri. LE11—4A 26
Grassington Clo. LE4—4H 3
Gravel St. LE1—3F 9
Graylyn Ct. LE4—2G 5
Grays Ct. LE9—1E 19
Gray St. LE2—5F 9
Gray St. LE11—4F 27
Gt. Arler Rd. LE2—3G 15
Gt. Central Rd. LE11—3G 27
Gt. Central St. LE1—3F 9
Gt. Meadow Rd. LE4—6G 3
Grebe Clo. LE3—2F 7
Greenacre Dri. LE5—4E 11
Greenbank Dri. LE2—6E 17
Greenbank Rd. LE5—1G 11
Greenclose La. LE11—2F 27
Greencoat Rd. LE3—2A 8
Greendale Rd. LE2—1C 20
Greenfields. LE8—5A 20
Greengate La. LE4—1A to 1C 4
Greenhill Rd. LE2—2H 15
Greenhithe Rd. LE2—2E 15
Greenland Av. LE5—2D 10
Greenland Dri. LE5—2D 10
Green La. LE8—2H 25
Green La. Clo. LE5—3C 10
Green La. Rd. LE5—3A to 3D 10
Greenside Pl. LE2—6F 15
Greensward. LE7—1D 28
Green, The. LE7—4A 28
Green,The. LE8—4D 20
Green, The. LE9—5A 24
(Croft)
Green, The. LE9—5C 18
(Huncote)
Green Wlk. LE3—4H 7
Greenway, The. LE4—6C 4
Greenwood Rd. LE5—3C 10
Gregory St. LE11—3G 27
Gregson Clo. LE4—3F 5
Grendon Clo. LE8—1C 22
Grenfell Hall. LE11—3D 26
Grenfell Rd. LE2—3C 16
Grenfell Wlk. LE2—3C 16
Gresley Clo. LE4—4H 3
Gretna Way. LE5—2H 11
Grey Clo. LE6—2B & 5A 2
Grey Friars. LE1—4F 9
Greyland Paddock. LE6—2B & 5A 2
Greystoke Clo. LE4—5B 4
Greystoke Wlk. LE4—5B 4
Greystone Av. LE5—4E 11
Griggs Rd. LE11—6F 27
Grisedale Clo. LE2—6F 9
Groby Rd. LE3—5B 2
(Glenfield)
Groby Rd. LE3—6E 3 to 2D 8
(Leicester)
Groby Rd. LE6—1B 6
Groby Rd. LE7—4C 2
Grocot Rd. LE5—6D 10
Grosvenor Cres. LE2—4C 16
Grosvenor St. LE1—3G 9
Grovebury Rd. LE4—5B 4
Grovebury Wlk. LE4—5B 4
Grove Rd. LE5—3A 10
Grove Rd. LE8—5B 20
Grove Rd. LE11—3D 26
Grove, The. LE11—3D 26
Guildhall La. LE1—4F 9
Guilford Dri. LE8—6H 15
Guilford Rd. LE2—2B 16
Guilford St. LE2—5A 10
Gullet La. LE9—5B 6
Gumley Sq. LE9—1F 19
Gunthorpe Rd. LE3—5H 7
Gurney Cres. LE9—6G 19
Guthlaxton St. LE2—5H 9
Guthridge Cres. LE3—6C 8
Gwencole Av. LE3—3B 14
Gwencole Cres. LE3—4B 14
Gwendolen Rd. LE5—4B 10
Gwendolen Rd. Gdns. LE5—5B 10
Gwendolin Av. LE4—1D 4
Gwendoline Dri. LE8—2G 25
Gynsill La. LE7—5D 2

Hackett Rd. LE3—1B 8
Haddenham Rd. LE3—1D 14
Haddon Clo. LE7—6A 28
Haddon St. LE2—4A 10
Hadrian Rd. LE4—3A 4
(Leicester)
Hadrian Rd. LE4—1F 5
(Thurmaston)
Hailey Av. LE11—1B 26
Haines Bldgs. LE3—4E 9
Halcroft Rise. LE8—3B 22
Half Moon Cres. LE2—4F 17
Halford St. LE1—4G 9
Halford St. LE7—5A 28
Halifax Dri. LE4—5A 4
Halkirk St. LE4—1H 9
Hallam Av. LE4—1C 4
Hallam Cres. E. LE3—1B & 1C 14
Hallaton Rd. LE5—2D 10
Hallaton St. LE2—4F 15
Hall Clo. LE2—1C 20
Hallcroft Av. LE8—2H 25
Hall Dri. LE2—4E 17
Hall La. LE2—4D 14
Hall Rd. LE7—1H 11
Hall Wlk. LE9—1F 19
Halsbury St. LE2—6A 10
Halstead St. LE5—4A 10
Hambledon Cres. LE11—6E 27
Hambledon Grn. LE4—3A 4
Hamble Rd. LE2—5F 17
Hamelin Rd. LE3—5A 8
Hamilford Clo. LE7—1H 11
Hamilton La. LE7—1H 11
Hamilton St. LE2—5H 9
Hammercliffe Rd. LE5—2A 10
Hampden Rd. LE4—6F 5
Hampshire Rd. LE2—3E 15
Hampton Clo. LE8—2C 22
Hanbury Rd. LE5—5G 11
Hand Av. LE3—6H 7
Handley St. LE2—4F 15
Hanover Clo. LE5—1E 11
Hanover Ct. LE11—2C 26
Harborough Rd. LE2—5D 16
Harcourt Clo. LE7—5A 28
Harcourt Rd. LE8—3B 22
Hardie Cres. LE3—1H 13
Harding St. LE1—3E 9
Harding Wlk. LE1—3E 9
Hardwick Cres. LE7—5A 28
Hardwick Dri. LE11—2C 26
Hardwick Rd. LE5—5G 11
Hardy's Av. LE4—4E 5
Harefield Av. LE3—3C 14
Harene Cres. LE3—6C 6
Harewood St. LE5—3B 10
Harland Clo. LE9—2B 24
Harlaxton St. LE3—1C 14
Harlech Clo. LE11—1D 26
Harold's La. LE9—6F 13
Harold St. LE2—3F 15
Harrington Rd. LE8—1C 22
Harrington St. LE4—2A 10
Harringworth Rd. LE5—5E 11
Harris Grn. LE3—6G 7
Harrison Rd. LE4—1H 9 to 5E 5
Harrison's Row. LE7—5A 28
Harrison St. LE4—1F 5
Harris Rd. LE4—5G 3
Harrogate Rd. LE4—1A 10
Harrowden Rise. LE5—3D 10
Harrow Rd. LE3—5D 8
Hartfield Rd. LE5—2F 11
Hartington Rd. LE2—4A 10
Hartopp Rd. LE2—1H 15
Hart Rd. LE5—3A 10
Hartshorn Clo. LE4—2H 5
Harvard Clo. LE2—5E 17
Harvest Clo. LE4—5G 3
Harvey Wlk. LE1—4F 9
Harwin Rd. LE5—5E 11
Hassal Rd. LE3—2A 8
Hastings Rd. LE5—2A 10
Hastings Rd. LE9—5D 6
Hastings St. LE11—2E 27
Hastings Wlk. LE3—2A 14
Hathaway Av. LE3—2A 14
Hatherleigh Rd. LE5—6C 10
Hathern Dri. LE11—1A 26
Hat Rd. LE3—3A 14
Hattern Av. LE4—4A 4
Havelock St. LE2—5F 9
Havelock St. LE11—2E 27
Havencrest Dri. LE5—2E 11
Haven Wlk. LE5—4H 11
Hawarden Av. LE5—3C 10
Hawkesbury Rd. LE2—4E 15
Hawkes Hill. LE2—5F 15
Hawthorn Clo. LE3—1D 12
Hawthorn Dri. LE5—6D 10
Hawthorn Dri. LE8—5C 20
Hawthorne. St. LE3—3D 8
Hawthorn Rise. LE6—3B & 5A 2
Hawthorns, The. LE8—1H 25
Hayden Clo. LE2—6G 17
Hayden Clo. LE4—5A 4
Haydon Rd. LE11—3D 26
Hayes Rd. LE8—1C 22
Hayling Cres. LE5—2D 10
Haymarket. LE1—3G 9
Haymarket Centre. LE1—3G 9
Haynes Rd. LE5—2C 10
Hayward Av. LE11—4H 27
Hazelbank Clo. LE4—6A 4
(in two parts)
Hazelbank Rd. LE8—1H 25
Hazel Clo. LE9—6G 19
Hazel Dri. LE3—4B 14
Hazelhead Rd. LE7—2C 2
Hazel Rd. LE11—6F 27
Hazel St. LE2—6F 9
Hazelwood Rd. LE5—6B 10
Hazelwood Rd. LE8—4G 21
Hazlerigg Hall. LE11—3D 26
Heacham Dri. LE4—5G 3 to 5A 4
Headland Rd. LE5—6D 10
Headland, The. LE7—1D 28
Headley Rd. LE3—4B 14
Healey St. LE8—3F 21
Healy Clo. LE4—4A 4
Heanor St. LE1—3F 9
Heard Wlk. LE4—4H 3
Heath Av. LE9—2H 19
Heathcoat St. LE11—3F 27
Heathcott Rd. LE2—4F 15
Heatherbrook Rd. LE4—3F 3
Heather Rd. LE2—3G 15
Heather Way. LE8—2H 25
Heathfield Rd. LE8—6B 16
Heathgate Clo. LE4—1B 4
Heays Clo. LE3—2A 8
Hebden Clo .LE2—2D 20
Heddington Clo. LE2—5H 15
Heddington Way. LE2—6H 15
Hedgerow La. LE9—4C 6
Hefford Gdns. LE4—4A 4
Heigton Cres. LE9—6G 19
Helena Cres. LE4—4B 4
Helmsley Rd. LE2—4F 15
Helston Clo. LE8—3A 22
Hemington Rd. LE5—6G 11
Henley Cres. LE3—2A 14
Henley Rd. LE3—4D 8
Henray Av. LE2—2D 20
Henshaw St. LE2—5F 9
Henson Clo. LE4—2B 4
Henton Rd. LE3—4D 8
Herbert Av. LE4—6D 4
Herbert Clo. LE8—5B 20
Herbert St. LE11—2F 27
Hereford Rd. LE2—4E 15
Hereward Dri. LE7—4H 11
Herle Av. LE3—1A 14
Herle Wlk. LE3—1A 14
Hermitage Clo. LE2—6D 16
Hermitage Rd. LE4—3C 4
Hermitage Rd. LE11—4B 26
(in two parts)
Heron Rd. LE5—3A 10
Heron's Way. LE7—1D 28
Heron Way. LE9—2H 19
Herrick Dri. LE7—4H 11
Herrick Rd. LE2—3G 15
Herrick Rd. LE11—5F 27
Herricks Av. LE4—3G 5
Herschell St. LE2—6A 10
Herthull Rd. LE5—3F 11
Hesilrige Wlk. LE5—1E 11
Hesketh Av. LE2—1D 20
Hesketh Clo. LE2—1D 20
Hewes Clo. LE2—1C 20
Hewitt Dri. LE9—5D 6
Hextall Rd. LE5—6D 10
Heybrook Av. LE8—5B 20
Heyford Rd. LE3—5H 7
Heythrop Clo. LE2—6F 17
Heyworth Rd. LE3—2D 14
Hidcote Rd. LE2—6D 16
Higgs Clo. LE5—4E 11
Highbury Rd. LE4—1A 10
Highcroft Av. LE2—6F 17
Highcroft Rd. LE2—1G 23
Highcross St. LE1—3F & 4F 9
Highfield Cres. LE8—1B 22
Highfield Dri. LE8—6B 16
Highfield Rd. LE6—3B 2
Highfields Dri. LE11—5C 26
Highfield St. LE2—5H 9
Highfield St. LE7—2D 2
Highgate. LE2—6G 15
Highgate Dri. LE2—5H 15
Highland Av. LE3—1D 12
High Leys Dri. LE2—6E 17
Highmeres Rd. LE4—5H 5
High St. LE1—4F 9
High St. LE2—5D 16
High St. LE5—1E 17
High St. LE7—4A 28
High St. LE8—4A 20
High St. LE9—1F 19
High St. LE11—3F 27
Highway Rd. LE4—1G 5
Highway Rd. LE5—1C 16
Hilary Cres. LE6—3A 2
Hilders Rd. LE3—3B 8
Hildyard Rd. LE4—1G 9
Hillary Pl. LE3—1B 14
Hillberry Clo. LE9—4E 19
Hill Ct. LE7—5H 11
Hillcrest Rd. LE2—5H 15
Hillcroft Clo. LE4—1G 5
Hillcroft Rd. LE5—5C 10
Hill La. LE8—2E 25
Hill Rise. LE4—1C 4
(Birstall)
Hill Rise. LE4—3H 5
(Thurmaston)
Hillrise Av. LE3—3B 14
Hillsborough Clo. LE2—2D 20
Hillsborough Cres. LE2—2D 20
Hillsborough Rd. LE2—2D 20
Hillside Av. LE8—3B 22
Hill St. LE1—3G 9
Hill St. LE9—5A 24
Hill Top Rd. LE11—6D 26
Hill View Dri. LE9—3B 24
Hill Way. LE2—1F 23
Hinckley Rd. LE9 & LE3—3A 12 to 5E 9
Hincks Av. LE7—1H 11
Hindoostan Av. LE8—2F 21
Hipwell Cres. LE4—5A 4
Hoball Clo. LE3—2A 8
Hobart St. LE2—5H 9
Hobill Clo. LE3—1F 13
Hobill Clo. LE9—4C 18
Hobson Rd. LE4—5B 4
Hoby St. LE3—3E 9
Hockley Farm Rd. LE3—5G 7
Hodgson Clo. LE3—1B 8
Holbrook Rd. LE2—3B 16
Holden St. LE4—6C 4
Holderness Rd. LE4—3H 3
Holgate Clo. LE7—1D 2
Holkham Av. LE4—1B 10
Holland Rd. LE2—3H 9
Hollies Way. LE7—5H 11
Hollington Rd. LE5—5B 10
Hollins Rd. LE3—5A 8
Hollow Rd. LE7—2D 2
Hollow, The. LE5—1E17
Hollybrook Clo. LE4—2H 5
Hollybush Clo. LE5—3G 11
Holly Gro. LE8—4C 20
Holly Tree Av. LE4—1C 4
Holmdale Rd. LE7—6A 28
Holmden Av. LE8—2H 21
Holme Dri. LE2—4E 17
Holmes Clo. LE6—2A 2
Holmewood Dri. LE9—5D 6
Holmfield Av. LE2—1B 16
Holmfield Av. LE11—1E 27
Holmfield Av. E. LE3—6G 7
Holmfield Av. W. LE3—6G 7
Holmfield Rd. LE2—1A 16
Holmleigh Gdns. LE7—5H 11
Holmrook Ho. LE2—1D 20
Holmwood Dri. LE3—1A 8
Holt Dri. LE9—5D 6
Holt Dri. LE11—5E 27
Holt Rd. LE4—3C 4
Holts Clo. LE2—6C 14
Holy Bones. LE1—4F 9
Holyoake St. LE9—2F 19
Holyrood Dri. LE8—2G 25
Holywell Dri. LE11—5C 26
Holywell Rd. LE2—5D 14
Home Clo. La. LE8—4C 20
Home Farm Clo. LE4—5H 3
Home Farm Sq. LE4—5H 3
Home Farm Wlk. LE4—5H 3
Homemead Av. LE4—5A 4
Homer Dri. LE9—4F 19
Homestead Dri. LE8—3B 22
Homestone Gdns. LE5—3H 11
Homestone Rise. LE5—3H 11
Homeway Rd. LE5—6B 10
Honeybourne Clo. LE2—6D 16
Honiton Clo. LE8—3A 22
Hopefield Rd. LE3—1D 14
Hopwood Clo. LE4—5G 3
Hopyard Clo. LE2—6C 14
Horndean Av. LE8—1A 22
Horsefair St. LE1—4F 9
Horsewell La. LE8—4B 22
Horston Rd. LE5—6B 10
Horwood Clo. LE8—6C 16
Hospital Clo. LE5—5D 10
Hospital La. LE8—5D 20
Hotel St. LE1—4F 9
Hotoft Rd. LE5—1E 11
Houghton St. LE5—2B 10
Houlditch Rd. LE2—3H 15
Housman Wlk. LE4—2H 9
Howard Clo. LE11—2B 26
Howard Rd. LE2—2C 20
(Glen Parva)
Howard Rd. LE2—2G 15
(Knighton)
Howard St. LE11—2F 27
Howden Clo. LE11—4A 26
Howden Rd. LE2—6D 14
(Aylestone)
Howden Rd. LE2—1E 23
(Oadby)
Howe Rd. LE11—6F 27
Hoylake Clo. LE5—1C 16
Hudson Clo. LE3—1B 8
Hudson St. LE11—2G 27
Huggett Clo. LE4—4F 5
Hughenden Dri. LE2—2F 15
Humber Clo. LE5—1E 11
Humberstone Dri. LE5—2D 10
Humberstone Ga. LE1—4G 9
Humberstone La. LE4—2F to 4G 5
Humberstone Rd. LE5 3G 9 to 2B 10
Humble La. LE7—1A 28
Hume St. LE11—2G 27
Humphries Clo. LE5—4D 10
Huncote Rd. LE9—5A 24 & 6A 18
(Croft)
Huncote Rd. LE9—5D 18
(Huncote)
Hungarton Boulevd. LE5—1E 11
Hunter Rd. LE4—1G 9
Hunters Way. LE2—6F 17
Huntingdon Rd. LE4—6F 5
Huntsman's Dale. LE7—1C 28
Huntsmans Way. LE4—5F 5
Hursley Clo. LE2—6F 17
Hurst Rise. LE5—4D 10
Hurstwood Rd. LE11—4B 26
Hutchinson St. LE2—4H 9
Hutchinson Wlk. LE2—4H 9
Hyde Clo. LE2—1F 23
Hydra Wlk. LE2—4H 9
Hylion Rd. LE2—5G 15

Ibbetson Av. LE3—3G 7
Ibsley Way. LE2—1E 21
Ickworth Clo. LE5—2B 10
Iffley Clo. LE5—4D 10
Iliffe Av. LE2—5C 16
Iliffe Rd. LE4—1B 10
Illingworth Rd. LE5—4E 11
Ilmington Clo. LE3—6C 2
Imperial Av. LE3—6C 8
Infirmary Clo. LE2—5F 9
Infirmary Rd. LE1—5F 9
Infirmary Sq. LE1—5F 9
Ingarsby Dri. LE5—6F 11
Ingleby Rd. LE8—1A 22
Ingle Dri. LE6—1B 6
Ingle St. LE3—3C 8
Ingold Av. LE4—5A 4
Invergarry Clo. LE4—4E 5
Iona Clo. LE4—5G 3
Iona Way. LE8—2H 25
Ireton Av. LE4—6G 5
Ireton Rd. LE4—6G 5
Iris Av. LE2—1C 20
Iris Av. LE4—1D 4
Irlam St. LE8—3G 21
Isis Clo. LE2—5G 17
Islington St. LE2—1F 15
Ivanhoe Clo. LE3—3G 7
Ivanhoe Rd. LE8—2F 21
Ivanhoe St. LE3—3D 8
Ivychurch Cres. LE5—1G 11
Ivydale Clo. LE4—2G 5
Ivydale Rd. LE4—2G 5
Ivy Rd. LE3—6D 8

Jacklin Dri. LE4—3F 5
Jackson St. LE4—5D 4
James Av. LE11—1B 26
James St. LE7—1D 2
James St. LE8—4C 20
Jamesway. LE9—2B 24
Jarett Clo. LE9—1E 19
Jarrom St. LE2—6F 9
Jarvis St. LE3—3E 9
Jean Dri. LE4—1E 9
Jellicoe Rd. LE5—4B 10
Jennett Clo. LE5—3F 11
Jeremy Clo. LE4—6D 4
Jermyn St. LE4—6D 4
Jersey Rd. LE4—4A 4
Jessons Clo. LE4—5F 5
Jessop Clo. LE3—1C 8
Jetcott Av. LE11—6E 27
Johns Ct. LE8—4C 20

Johnson Clo. LE8—5B 20
Johnson Rd. LE4—2C 4
Johnson St. LE1—3F 9
John St. LE2—2F 19
Jonathan Clo. LE6—5A 2
Jordan Av. LE8—3G 21
Journeyman's Grn. LE6—1C
Jowett Clo. LE3—1B 8
Joyce Rd. LE3—2C 8
Jubilee Cres. LE9—4G 19
Jubilee Dri. LE3—2G 7
Jubilee Dri. LE11—1E 27
Jubilee Rd. LE3—3G 9
Judges St. LE11—3H 27
Judith Dri. LE3—5E 11
Judith Rd. LE8—1H 25
Julian Rd. LE2—2D 20
Junction Rd. LE1—1F 13
Juction Rd. LE8—1B 22
June Av. LE4—3H 5
Junior St. LE1—3F 9
Jupiter Clo. LE2—4H 9

Kamloops Cres. LE1—3G 9
Kashmir Rd. LE1—3H 9
Kate St. LE3—4E 9
Kay Rd. LE3—2B 8
Keats Clo. LE9—2E 19
Keats Wlk. LE4—1H 9
Keats Way. LE11—1C 26
Keays Way. LE7—1H 11
Keble Dri. LE7—6B 28
Keble Rd. LE2—2G 15
Kedleston Av. LE4—3C 4
Kedleston Rd. LE5—6A 10
Keenan Clo. LE2—6C 14
Keepers' Croft. LE7—2D 28
Keepers Wlk. LE5—5G 3
Keep, The. LE9—4C 6
Kegworth Av. LE4—4C 10
Keightley Rd. LE3—1A 8
Keightley Wlk. LE4—2H 5
Kelbrook Clo. LE4—4B 4
Kelmarsh Av. LE8—2B 22
Kelso Grn. LE2—1E 21
Kelvon Clo. LE3—1H 7
Kemp Rd. LE3—1A 8
Kempson Rd. LE3—3F 15
Kendall's Av. LE9—6A 24
Kendal Rd. LE4—5F 5
Kendrick Rd. LE2—6E 17
Kenilworth Av. LE11—2B 26
Kenilworth Clo. LE5—5C 16
Kenilworth Rd. LE3—3B 14
Kennedy Way. LE3—1F 13
Kenneth Gamble Ct. LE8—1H 21
Kensington Av. LE11—2B 26
Kensington Clo. LE2—3E 21
(Glen Parva)
Kensington Clo. LE6—6A 16
(Oadby)
Kensington St. LE4—1G 9
Kent Cres. LE2—2F 21
(in two parts)
Kent Dri. LE2—6H 15
(Knighton)
Kent Dri. LE2—5F 17
(Oadby)
Kenton Av. LE8—3A 22
Kent St, LE5 & LE2—3H 9
Kenwood Rd. LE2—4A 16
Kepston Clo. LE2—2B 20
Kernan Dri. LE11—1E 27
Kerrial Gdns. LE3—2H 7
Kerrial Rd. LE3—2H 7
Kerrysdale Av. LE4—3H 5
Kestrel Clo. LE5—3A 10
Keswick Av. LE11—5C 26
Keswick Clo. LE4—1D 4
Keswick Rd. LE8—5C 20
Kevern Clo. LE8—3A 22
Kew Dri. LE2—1F 23
Keyham Clo. LE5—1E 11
Keyham La. LE5—1E to 1G 11
Keyham La. W. LE5—1G 11
Keythorpe St. LE2—4H 9
Kilburn Av. LE2—5D 16
Kilby Av. LE4—3C 4
Kilby Dri. LE8—3B 22
Kildare St. LE1—3G 9
Kilmelford Clo. LE4—4F 5

Kiln Av. LE4—2H 5
Kilverstone Av. LE5—6G 11
Kilworth Dri. LE5—6C 10
Kimberley Rd. LE2—6A 10
Kincaple Rd. LE4—4F 5
Kincraig Rd. LE4—4F 5
King Edward Av. LE9—4F 19
King Edward Rd. LE5—2C 10
King Edward Rd. LE11—3G 27
Kingfisher Av. LE5—3A 10
Kingfisher Wlk. LE5—3A 10
King George Av. LE11—4H 27
King George Rd. LE11—4H 27
King Richard's Rd. LE3—4E 9
Kings Av. LE11—1E 27
Kingsbury Av. LE5—5F 11
Kingscliffe Cres. LE5—5G 11
Kingsley Clo. LE4—1B 4
Kingsley St. LE2—2G 15
Kings Lock Clo. LE2—6C 14
Kingsmead Rd. LE2—4A 16
Kings Newton St. LE2—5A 10
Kingsthorpe Clo. LE4—5B 4
Kingston Av. LE8—6H 15
Kingston Rd. LE2—6A 10
King St. LE1—5G 9
King St. LE2—5E 17
King St. LE5—5B 20
King St. LE9—1F 19
King St. LE11—3G 27
Kings Wlk. LE3—6F 7
Kingsway. LE3—2A to 4B 14
Kingsway N. LE3—1H 13
Kingsway Rd. LE5—1B 16
Kingswood Av. LE3—5D 8
King William's Way. LE7—2E 3
Kinley Rd. LE4—4B 4
Kinross Av. LE5—4H 11
Kinross Cres. LE11—2C 26
Kinsdale Rd. LE5—3H 11
Kintyre Dri. LE4—4E 5
Kipling Dri. LE2—2E 19
Kipling Gro. LE4—5G 3
Kirby La. LE6—6D 6
Kirby Rd. LE3—4D 8
Kirby Rd. LE9 & LE3—2E 7
Kirke Wlk. LE3—4H 7
Kirkfield Rd. LE8—1H 25
Kirkland Rd. LE3—3B 14
Kirk La. LE9—1G 19
Kirkscroft Wlk. LE4—5B 4
Kirkstead Wlk. LE4—5B 4
Kirkstone Clo. LE11—3G 27
Kirkstone Clo. LE2—2H 7
Kirkwall Cres. LE5—2H 11
Kirloe Av. LE3—6E 7
Kirminton Gdns. LE5—3F 11
Kitchener Rd. LE5—4B 10
Kitchener Rd. LE7—2D 2
Knight Grange Rd. LE2—2B 16
Knighton Church Rd. LE2
—3A 16
Knighton Ct. LE2—1A 16
Knighton Dri. LE2—2A 16
Knighton Fields Rd. E. LE2
—3G 15
Knighton Fields Rd. W. LE2
—2F 15
Knighton Hall. LE2—3A 16
Knighton Junction La. LE2
—2G 15
Knighton La. LE2—3F 15
Knighton La. E. LE2—3F 15
Knighton Lodge. LE2—2A 16
Knighton Pk. Rd. LE2—1H 15
Knighton Rise. LE2—2C 16
Knighton Rd. LE2—3H 15 to
2B 16
Knighton St. LE2—6F 9
Knightsbridge Rd. LE2—3E 21
Knighthorpe Ct. LE11—2C 26
Knighthorpe Rd. LE11—2C 26
Knollgate Clo. LE4—4G 26
Knowles Rd. LE3—2A 8
Knowle, The. LE3—3A 16
Krefeld Rd. LE4—5F 3

Labrador Clo. LE1—3H 9
Laburnam Rd. LE5—1F 11
Ladbroke Gro. LE8—1H 25
Ladybower Rd. LE11—4B 26
Lady Leys. LE9—3A 24
Ladysmith Rd. LE2—2F 21
Ladysmith Rd. LE9—4C 6
Lakeside Ct. LE7—5H 11
Lambert Rd. LE3—1D 14
Lambourne Rd. LE2—5H 15
Lambourne Rd. LE4—1D 4
Lamen Rd. LE3—1A 8
Lamport Clo. LE8—2C 22
Lamport Clo. LE11—2B 26
Lancashire St. LE4—5D 4
Lancaster Rd. LE1—6G 9
(in two parts)
Lancaster St. LE5—4B 10
Lancaster Way. LE2—3E 21
Lancing Av. LE3—3B 8
Landscape Dri. LE5—5F 11
Landseer Rd. LE2—6H 15
Lane Clo. LE3—2G 7
Lanesborough Rd. LE4—4D 4
Laneshaw Av. LE11—4A 26
Langdale Av. LE11—5C 26
Langdale Ho. LE12—1D 28
Langdale Rd. LE4—2C 5
Langham Dri. LE4—4F 19
Langhill, The. LE5—4C 10
(in two parts)
Langholm Rd. LE5—4H 11
Langley Av. LE4—2H 5
Langley Clo. LE9—4C 18
Langley Wlk. LE4—5B 4
Langton Rd. LE8—3B 22
Lansdowne Dri. LE11—5F 27
Lansdowne Gro. LE8—4G 21
Lansdowne Rd. LE2—3F 15
Larch Gro. LE3—6G 7
Larch St. LE5—2A 10
Larchwood. LE8—1H 25
Lastingham Clo. LE2—4G 15
Latimer Clo. LE8—5B 20
Latimer St. LE3—5D 8
Latimer St. LE7—3D 2
Launceston Rd. LE8—3A 22
Launde Rd. LE2—4F 17
Laundry La. LE4—5D 4
Laurel Clo. LE3—2H 7
Laurel Dri. LE2—1G 23
Laurel Rd. LE8—1H 25
Laurel Rd. LE5—5A 10
Laurel Rd. LE8—6D 20
Laureston Dri. LE2—1A 16
Lavender Clo. LE8—4C 20
Lavender Rd. LE4—5B 4
Laverstock Rd. LE8—4A 22
Lawford Rd. LE2—6D 14
Lawn Av. LE4—1D 4
Lawnwood Rd. LE6—2A 2
Lawrence Kershaw Hall. LE2
—5F 9
Lawrence Wlk. LE3—5B 4
Lawrence Way. LE11—1B 26
Law St. LE4—1G 9
Lawyers La. LE2—6D 16
(in two parts)
Laxford Clo. LE4—6H 3
Laxton Clo. LE4—1D 4
Laxton Clo. LE8—2C 22
Layton Rd. LE5—2B 10
Lea Clo. LE4—1F 5
Leamington Dri. LE8—6C 20
Leckhampton Rd. LE2—4A 16
Leconfield Rd. LE11—6B 26
Ledbury Clo. LE2—6E 17
Ledbury Grn. LE4—3H 3
Ledbury Rd. LE11—6E 27
Ledwell Dri. LE3—1G 7
Lee Rise LE6—2C 6
Leeson St. LE2—4F 15
Lee St. LE1—3G 9
Leicester La. LE9—2A 12
(Desford)
Leicester La. LE9—1F 19
(Enderby)
Leicester Rd. LE2—3C to 5D 16
Leicester Rd. LE8—6D 2
Leicester Rd. LE4—1A 4
Leicester Rd. LE6—2B & 5A to
5B 2

Leicester Rd. LE7—3D 2
Leicester Rd. LE8—6A 16
Leicester Rd. LE8 & LE2—3C 20
(in two parts)
Leicester Rd. LE4—4G to 2H 19
Leicester Rd. LE11 & LE12
—3G 27
Leicester St. LE5—3B 10
Leire St. LE4—6D 4
Lema Clo. LE4—4H 5
Lemyngton St. LE11—2G 27
Lena Dri. LE6—1A 2
Leopold Clo. LE2—6G 25
Leopold Rd. LE2—4G 15
Leopold St. LE8—3F 21
Leopold St. LE11—2E 27
Leslie Clo. LE11—1C 26
Letchworth Rd. LE3—3B & 4B 8
Lethbridge Clo. LE1—3G 9
Leveric Rd. LE5—1C 10
Lewis Clo. LE4—5G 3
Lewis Rd. LE11—1C 26
Lewis Way. LE8—2H 25
Lewitt Clo. LE4—4A 4
Lexham St. LE4—6D 4
Leybury Way. LE7—3H 11
Leycroft Rd. LE4—2G 3
Leyland Rd. LE3—4B 14
Leys Clo. LE2—4E 17
Leysdale Clo. LE4—5G 3
Leys, The. LE7—6B 28
Leys, The. LE8—2F 25
Liberty Rd. LE3—2B 8
Lichfield Dri. LE8—6C 20
Lichfield St. LE1—5F 9
Lidster Clo. LE5—1E 11
Lilac Av. LE3—2H 7
Lilac Wlk. LE5—1F 11
Limber Cres. LE3—6A 8
Lime Av. LE11—4G 27
Lime Cres. LE7—6B 28
Lime Gro. LE8—6D 20
Lime Gro. LE9—5C 6
Lime Gro. Clo. LE4—4H 3
Limehurst Av. LE11—2F 27
Limehurst Rd. LE5—1G 11
Limetree Rd. LE9—2H 19
Linacres Rd. LE3—6A 8
Lincoln Dri. LE8—6D 2
(Blaby)
Lincoln Dri. LE8—2G 21
(Wigston)
Lincoln St. LE2—5H 9
Linden Clo. LE8—2F 25
Linden Dri. LE5—6D 10
Linden Farm Dri. LE8—1G 25
Linden La. LE9—6D 6
Linden Rd. LE11—2F 27
Linden St. LE5—4B 10
Lindfield Rd. LE3—3B 8
Lindrick Dri. LE5—1C 16
Lindsay Rd. LE2—2C 14
Linford Clo. LE8—2C 22
Linford Rd. LE11—6D 26
Linford St. LE4—5D 4
Ling Av. LE11—6G 27
Ling Dale. LE7—1D 28
Ling Rd. LE11—6G 27
Link Rd. LE2—4B 16
Link Rd. LE7—2C 2
(Anstey)
Link Rd. LE7—4C 28
(Queniborough)
Links Rd. LE8—5B 6
Linkway Gdns. LE3—5D 8
Linley Grn. LE9—3B 24
Linney Rd. LE4—5H 3
Lintlaw Clo. LE4—4F 5
Linton St. LE5—6A 10
Linwood La. LE2—5G 15
Lisle St. LE11—2C 27
Lismore Wlk. LE5—5G 3
Litelmede. LE5—2C 10
Little Av. LE4—5D 4
Lit. Barley Clo. LE4—5G 3
Littlegarth. LE2—6G 15
Lit. Glen Rd. LE2—3D 20
Lit. Hill. LE8—2B 22
Lit. Holme St. LE3—4E 9
Littlejohn Rd. LE2—6E 15
Little La. LE1—4F 9

Lit. Moor La. LE11—3H 27
Littlemore Clo. LE5—4D 10
Littleton St. LE4—2E 9
Littleway,The. LE5—3C 10
(in two parts)
Lit. Wood Clo. LE4—4H 3
Livingstone St. LE3—5D 8
Lobbs Wood Clo. LE5—2E 11
Locke Av. LE4—3F 5
Lockerbie Av. LE4—4E 5
Lockerbie Wlk. LE4—4F 5
Lockhouse Clo. LE2—6C 14
Lodge Clo. LE7—5B 28
Lodge Clo. LE9—4C 18
Lodge Farm Rd. LE5—4F 11
Lodgewood Av. LE4—1C 4
Logan Av. LE2—4D 14
Lombardy Rise. LE5—2A 10
Lomond Cres. LE4—5H 3
London Rd. LE2—5G 9 to 3C 16
(Leicester)
London Rd. LE2—5E 17
(Oadby)
London Rd. LE2 & LE8—2G &
2H 23
London St. LE5—3B & 4B 10
Longcliffe Gdns. LE11—6A 26
Longcliffe Rd. LE5—2A 10
Longfellow Rd. LE2—1E 19
Longford Clo. LE8—3A 22
Long Furrow. LE7—2C 28
Long La. LE1—3F 9
Long La. LE8—2B 22
Longleat Clo. LE5—1B 10
Longstone Grn. LE5—3G 11
Long St. LE8—2A 22
Lonsdale Rd. LE4—2F 5
Lonsdale St. LE2—5A 10
Lord Byron St. LE2—2G 15
Lorne Rd. LE2—2H 15
Lorraine Rd. LE2—4F 15
Lorrimer Rd. LE2—2H 15
Loseby La. LE1—4F 9
Lothair Rd. LE2—2F 15
Loughborough Rd. LE4—6D
to 1C 4
Loughborough Rd. LE11—6H 27
Lowcroft Dri. LE2—6F 17
Lwr. Brown St. LE1—5F 9
Lwr. Cambridge St. LE1
—1F 27
Lwr. Church St. LE7—4A 28
Lwr. Gladstone St. LE11—2F 27
Lwr. Hill St. LE1—3G 9
Lwr. Lee St. LE1—3G 9
Lwr. Willow St. LE1—2G 9
Loweswater Dri. LE11—5C 26
Lowick Dri. LE8—2C 22
Lowland Av. LE3—1E 13
Loxley Rd. LE3—1G 7
Lubbesthorpe Bridle Rd. LE3
—2A 14
Lubbesthorpe Rd. LE3—4A 14
Ludgate Clo. LE4—1B 4
Ludlow Clo. LE2—6F 17
Ludlow Clo. LE11—6C 26
Lulworth Clo. LE5—5D 10
Lulworth Clo. LE8—5B 22
Lunsford Rd. LE5—2A 10
Luther St. LE3—5D 8
Lutterworth Rd. LE2—6D 14
Lutterworth Rd. LE8 & LE8
—6C 24 to 4C 20
Lyall Clo. LE11—1C 26
Lydall Rd. LE2—6E 15
Lydford Rd. LE4—5G 5
Lyme Rd. LE2—6A 10
Lymington Rd. LE5—1G 11
Lyncote Rd. LE3—2C 14
Lyndale Clo. LE2—2C 14
Lyndale Rd. LE3—3A 14
Lyndhurst Rd. LE2—4D 16
Lyndon Dri. LE2—4C 16
Lyngate Av. LE1—1C 4
Lynholme Rd. LE2—5F 15
Lynmouth Dri. LE8—6H 15
Lynmouth Rd. LE5—1G 11
Lyon Clo. LE8—6H 15
Lytham Rd. LE2—4F 15
Lytton Rd. LE2—1H 15

Macaulay St. LE2—2G 15

Macdonald Rd. LE4—1G 9
McKenzie Wlk. LE5—4D 10
Mackenzie Way. LE1—3G 9
Maclean Av. LE11—1C 26
McVicker Clo. LE5—4D 10
Madras Rd. LE1—3H 9
Magna Rd. LE8—3G 21
Magnolia Clo. LE2—5D 14
Maidstone Rd. LE2—4H 9
Maidwell Clo. LE8—2C 22
Main St. LE3—1A 14
(Braunstone)
Main St. LE3—1F 7
(Glenfield)
Main St. LE1—1E 17
(Evington)
Main St. LE1—1E 11
(Humberstone)
Main St. LE8—1B 6
Main St. LE7—2H 11
(Scraptoft)
Main St. LE7—5H 11
(Thurnby)
Main St. LE8—3B 24
(Cosby)
Main St. LE9—5C 18
(Huncote)
Main St. LE9—4C 6
(Kirby Muxloe)
Main St. LE2—2A 18
(Thurlaston)
Malabar Rd. LE1—3H 9
Malcolm Arc. LE1—4F 9
Malham Clo. LE4—4H 3
Mallard Av. LE6—3B 2
Mallory Pl. LE5—1C 10
Malton Dri. LE2—5F 17
Malvern Cres. LE9—3B 24
Malvern Rd. LE2—1B 16
Mandervell Rd. LE2—5C 16
Mandora La. LE2—5H 9
Manitoba Rd. LE1—3G 9
Manners Rd. LE2—3F 15
Manor Dri. LE2—3E 17
Manor Dri. LE3—3F 3
Manor Rd. LE11—6G 27
Manor Gdns. LE3—2G 7
Manor Rd. LE2—3D 16
Manor Rd. LE2—2F 5
Manor Rd. LE9—1B 24
Manor Rd. LE11—6C 26
Manor Rd. Extension. LE2
—3E 17
Mansfield St. LE1—3H 9
Mantle Rd. LE3—3D 8
Maple Av. LE3—6G 7
Maple Av. LE8—5C 20
(Blaby)
Maple Av. LE8—1H 25
(Countesthorpe)
Maple Clo. LE6—6B 4
Maple Rd. LE4—2F 5
Maple Rd. LE11—6F 27
Maple Rd. N. LE11—6F 27
Maple Rd. S. LE11—6F 27
Mapleton Rd. LE8—1A 22
Maplewell Dri. LE4—2F 3
Maplin Rd. LE5—1G 11
Marble St. LE1—4F 9
Mardale Way. LE11—6C 26
Marfitt St. LE4—5D 4
Margaret Clo. LE4—1F 5
Margaret Cres. LE8—1B 6
Margaret Rd. LE5—5B & 4B 10
Marina Dri. LE8—5B 6
Marina Rd. LE5—5B 10
Marjorie St. LE4—6D 4
Market Pl. LE1—4F 9
Market Pl. LE11—3F 27
Market Pl. App. LE1—4G 9
Market Pl. S. LE1—4F 9
Market St. LE1—4F 9
Market St. LE11—3F 27
Markfield Rd. LE6—1A to 2B 2
(Groby)
Markfield Rd. LE6—1B 6
(Ratby)
Markland. LE2—6D 14
Marlborough St. LE1—5F 9
Marlow Rd. LE3—1D 14

Maromme Sq. LE8—1B 22
Marquis St. LE1—5G 9
Marriott Rd. LE2—5F 15
Marsden Av. LE7—3C 28
Marsden La. LE2—4C 14
Marshall St. LE3—2E 9
Marsh Clo. LE4—3G 5
Marston Clo. LE2—1E 23
Marston Cres. LE8—2H 25
Marston Dri. LE6—5A 2
Marston Rd. LE4—6F 5
Marston Rd. LE9—5A 24 &
        6A 18
Marstown Av. LE2—2F 21
Martin Av. LE2—5E 17
Martin Av. LE3—6D 6
Martin Clo. LE4—1H 9
Martindale Clo. LE2—6F 9
Martinshaw La. LE6—2A 2
Martin St. LE4—1H 9
Martival. LE5—2C 10
Marwell Clo. LE4—4B 4
Marwell Wlk. LE4—4B 4
Marwood Rd. LE4—4A 4
Marydene Dri. LE5—6F 11
Mary Gee Houses. LE2—2A 16
Mary Rd. LE3—2C 8
Masefield Av. LE9—2F 19
Matlock Av. LE8—3G 21
Matlock St. LE2—4A 10
Matts Clo. LE2—5E 15
Maurice Dri. LE8—2G 25
Mavis Av. LE3—1D 14
Maxfield Ho. LE2—4H 9
Maxwell Dri. LE11—1B 26
Mayfield Dri. LE8—6B 16
Mayfield Rd. LE11—4F 27
Mayfield Rd. LE2—6A 10
Mayflower Rd. LE5—6C 10
Maynard Rd. LE2—4H 9
Mayo Clo. LE11—6E 27
Mayor's Wlk. LE1—6G 9
Maytree Clo. LE3—4B 4
Maytree Ct. LE3—6C 6
Maytree Dri. LE3—6C 6
Meadhurst Rd. LE3—4C 8
Meadow Av. LE11—1G 27
Meadow Clo. LE8—2C 6
Meadow Ct. LE2—4D 14
Meadowcourt Rd. LE2—4C 16
Meadow Dri. LE6—5A 2
Meadow Gdns. LE2—5G 15
Meadow La. LE4—1D 4
Meadow La. LE11—2G 27
Meadows, The. LE7—1D 28
Meadow View. LE6—3G 3
Meadow Way. LE6—3B & 5A 2
Meadow Way. LE8—2C 22
Meads, The. LE3—4A 8
Meadvale Rd. LE2—4H 15
Meadway. LE3—3B 8
Meadway, The. LE4—1C 4
Meadway, The. LE7—6A 28
Meadwell Rd. LE3—5G 7
Medina Rd. LE3—2D 8
Medway St. LE2—5A 10
Melbourne Rd. LE2—5A 10
Melbourne St. LE2—4H 9
Melbreak Av. LE11—6D 26
Melcombe Wlk. LE4—5B 4
Melcroft Av. LE3—4C 8
Melford St. LE5—2C 10
Melland Pl. LE2—2D 20
Mellerstain Wlk. LE5—2B 10
Mellor Rd. LE3—4B 8
Melrose St. LE4—1H 9
Melton Av. LE4—3E 5
Melton Rd. LE4—6D 4 to 1F 5
Melton Rd. LE4—6A to 2D 28
Melton St. LE1—2G 9
Memory La. LE1—2G 9
Mendip Av. LE4—1D 8
Mensa Clo. LE4—1D 8
Mercer's Way. LE7—2D 28
Merchant's Comn. LE7—2D 28
Mercia Rd. LE2—5C 16
Mercury Clo. LE4—4F 5
Mere Clo. LE5—3A 10
Meredith Rd. LE3—2C 14
Mere Rd. LE5—5A to 3A 10
Mere Rd. LE8—6H 25
  (Peatling Magna)

Mere Rd. LE8—1C 22
  (Wigston)
Mereworth Clo. LE5—2B 10
Merton Av. LE3—4D 8
Merton Dri. LE7—6B 28
Merton Ho. LE5—3D 10
Mervyn Rd. LE5—6B 10
Methuen Av. LE4—1G 5
Meynall Rd. LE2—6F 17
Meynell Rd. LE5—3B 10
Mickleton Dri. LE5—6E 11
Middle Av. LE11—1E 27
Middlesex Rd. LE2—4E 15
Middleton Clo. LE8—2C 22
Middleton Pl. LE11—5F 27
Middleton St. LE2—4D 14
Midhurst Av. LE3—2A 14
Midland Cotts. LE8—2H 21
Midland St. LE1—4G 9
Midway Rd. LE5—3A 10
Mildenhall Rd. LE11—2B 26
Milford Clo. LE6—4F 3
Milford Rd. LE2—3H 15
Mill Av. LE4—1F 5
Millbrook Clo. LE4—5B 4
Millbrook Wlk. LE4—5B 4
Mill Clo. LE8—4G 21
Mill Dri. LE6—2C 6
Miller Clo. LE4—3G 5
Millers Clo. LE3—1F 7
Millers Clo. LE7—6A 28
Millersdale Av. LE5—5G 11
Millfield Clo. LE7—3D 2
Millfield Cres. LE3—4A 14
Mill Hill. LE4—5C 4
Mill Hill. LE9—6E 13
Mill Hill Clo. LE8—4B 20
Mill Hill La. LE2—5H 9
Milligan Rd. LE2—4E 15
Mill La. LE2—5F 9
Mill La. LE8—4D 20
Mill La. LE9—1F 19
Mill La. LE11—2G 27
Mill La., The. LE3—1E 7
Millstone La. LE1—4F 9
Millstone La. LE2—4C 28
Mill St. LE1—5F 9
Mills Yd. LE11—3F 27
Millwood Clo. LE4—3A 4
Milnroy Rd. LE5—3H 11
Milton Clo. LE8—2C 22
Milton Cres. LE4—5G 3
Milton Gdns. LE2—6E 17
Milton St. LE3—3E 9
Milton St. LE11—1D 26
Milverton Av. LE4—6H 3
Milverton Dri. LE6A 16
Minehead St. LE3—6A 8
Minster Cres. LE4—6A 4
Minstrel's Wlk. LE7—1D 28
Mitchell Rd. LE9—1E 19
Moat Rd. LE5—4B 10
Moat Rd. LE11—6D 26
Moat St. LE8—2A 22
Modbury Av. LE4—4A 4
Moira St. LE4—6D 4
Moira St. LE11—3G 27
Monarch Clo. LE4—1E 5
Monckton Clo. LE1—2G 9
Monica Rd. LE3—4B 14
Monmouth Dri. LE2—2D 20
Monsarrat Way. LE11—1C 26
Monsell Dri. LE2—5D 14
Montague Av. LE8—6B 28
Montague Rd. LE2—1H 15
Montreal Rd. LE1—3F 9
Montrose Clo. LE5—1D 10
Montrose Rd. LE2—5D 14
Montrose Rd. S. LE2—5D 14
Moon Clo. LE4—4H 9
Moon Wlk. LE4—4H 9
Moores La. LE9—1F 19
Moores Rd. LE4—6D 4
Moorfields. LE5—1G 11
Moorgate Av. LE4—1B 4
Moorgate St. LE4—1G 5
Moor La. LE11—3G & 3H 27
Morban Rd. LE2—5C 14
Morcote Rd. LE3—6A 8
Morland Av. LE2—3B 16
Morledge St. LE1—4G 9

Morley Rd. LE5—3A 10
Morley St. LE11—2G 27
Mornington St. LE5—3B 10
Morpeth Av. LE4—3H 3
Morris Hall. LE11—3D 26
Morris Rd. LE2—2G 15
Mortimer Pl. LE3—2C 14
Mortimer Rd. LE8—5E 19
Mortimer Way. LE3—2C 14
Mortoft Rd. LE4—5D 4
Morton Wlk. LE5—2B 10
Morwoods, The. LE2—5E 17
Mossdale Clo. LE2—6F 9
Mossdale Rd. LE3—3A 14
Mosse Way. LE2—5F 17
Mossgate. LE3—3C 8
Mostyn Av. LE2—4B 28
Mostyn St. LE3—4E 9
Mottisford Rd. LE4—4B 4
Mottisford Wlk. LE4—4B 4
Mount Av. LE5—3B 10
Mountcastle Rd. LE3—1D 14
Mountfields Dri. LE11—4D 26
Mount Rd. LE2—5E 17
Mount Rd. LE5—3A 10
Mount Rd. LE9—2B 24
Mount, The. LE7—1H 11
Mowbray Dri. LE7—5C 28
Mowmacre Hill. LE4—3B 4
Mowsley End. LE8—2B 22
Mulberry Av. LE3—3G 7
Mull Way. LE8—2H 25
Mumford Hall. LE11—4C 26
Mundella St. LE2—6A 10
Munnings Clo. LE4—4F 5
Murdoch Rise. LE11—1C 26
Muriel Rd. LE3—4D 8
Murrayfield Rd. LE3—5G 7
Murray St. LE2—4H 9
Museum Sq. LE5—5G 9
Musgrove Clo. LE3—4A 8
Musson Rd. LE2—2A 8
Myrtle Rd. LE2—5A 10

Nagle Gro. LE4—3F 5
Namur Rd. LE8—1F 21
Nanpanton Rd. LE11—6B 26
Nansen Rd. LE5—5C 10
Narborough Rd. LE3—2C 14 to
        5E 9
Narborough Rd. LE9—1A 24
  (Cosby)
Narborough Rd. LE9—5C 18
  (Huncote)
Narborough Rd. N. LE3—5E 9
Narborough Rd. S. LE9 & LE3
  —6A to 2C 14
Narrow La. LE2—4D 14
Naseby Clo. LE8—2C 22
Naseby Dri. LE11—4A 26
Naseby Rd. LE4—6G 5
Navigation St. LE4—6D 4
Naylor Av. LE11—4H 27
Naylor Rd. LE7—4B 28
Neal Av. LE3—1H 13
Necton St. LE7—5A 28
Nedham St. LE2—3H 9
Needham Av. LE2—2B 20
Needlegate. LE1—3F 9
Nelot Way. LE5—5E 11
Nelson St. LE1—5G 9
Nelson St. LE7—6A 28
Nene Ct. LE2—5F 17
Nene Dri. LE2—5F 17
Neptune Clo. LE2—4A 10
Neston Gdns. LE2—4G 15
Neston Rd. LE2—4G 15
Netherfield Rd. LE7—1D 2
Netherhall La. LE4—2A 10
Nether Hall Rd. LE5—1F 11
Netton Clo. LE8—4A 22
Navanthon Rd. LE3—4C 8
Neville Rd. LE3—4C 8
Newarke Clo. LE2—5F 9
Newarke St. LE1—4F 9
Newarke, The. LE2—5F 9
Newark Rd. LE4—2F 5
New Ashby Rd. LE11—5A 26
New Bond St. LE1—4F 9
New Bri. Rd. LE2—2C 20
New Bri. St. LE2—6F 9
Newbury Clo. LE8—3A 22

Newcombe Rd. LE3—1C 14
New Fields Av. LE3—1B 14
New Fields Sq. LE3—2C 14
New Forest Clo. LE8—4B 22
New Forest Rd. LE8—4B 22
Newgate End. LE8—2A 22
Newhaven Rd. LE5—6F 11
New Henry St. LE3—3E 9
Newington St. LE4—6D 4
Newington Wlk. LE4—6D 4
New King St. LE11—3G 27
Newlyn Pde. LE5—1G 11
Newmarket St. LE2—3H 15
New Pk. Rd. LE2—3F 15
New Parks Boulevd. LE3—4H 7
        to 1B 8
New Parks Cres. LE3—2C 8
New Pk. St. LE3—4E 9
New Parliament St. LE1—3G 9
New Pingle St. LE3—3E 9
Newport Pl. LE1—4G 9
Newport St. LE3—3D 8
Newquay Dri. LE3—6C 2
New Rd. LE1—3F 9
New Romney Clo. LE5—2G 11
New Romney Cres. LE5—1G 11
Newry, The. LE2—6G 15
New Star Rd. LE4—5H 5
Newstead Av. LE3—1D 8
Newstead Rd. LE8—6A 16
Newstead Rd. LE2—3A 16
New St. LE1—4F 9
New St. LE2—4E & 5E 17
New St. LE4—4D 28
New St. LE8—3C 20
  (Blaby)
New St. LE8—2H 25
  (Countesthorpe)
New St. LE11—3F 27
Newton Clo. LE11—1C 26
Newton La. LE8—2B 22 to
        5G 23
Newtown Linford La. LE6—1B &
        4A 2
Newtown St. LE1—5G 9
New Wlk. LE1—5G & 5H 9
New Wlk. Centre. LE1—5F 9
New Way Rd. LE5—1B 16
New Zealand La. LE7—3C 28
Nicholas Dri. LE6—2B 6
Nichols St. LE1—4H 9
Nicklaus Rd. LE4—4F 5
Nidderdale Rd. LE8—2C 22
Noble St. LE3—4D 8
Noel St. LE3—6D 8
Nook Clo. LE6—3B 6
Nook St. LE3—3C 8
Nook, The. LE7—2D 2
Nook, The. LE8—5B 20
Nook, The. LE9—3B 24
  (Cosby)
Nook, The. LE9—1F 19
  (Enderby)
Norbury Av. LE4—6A 4
Norfolk Rd. LE8—1F 21
Norfolk St. LE3—4D 8
Norfolk Wlk. LE3—4E 9
Norman Rd. LE4—1F 5
Norman St. LE3—5E 9
Normanton Rd. LE5—5A 10
Norris Clo. LE4—3G 5
Northampton Sq. LE1—4G 9
Northampton St. LE1—4G 9
  (in two parts)
North Av. LE2—1A 16
N. Bridge Pl. LE3—2E 9
Northcote Rd. LE2—3H 15
Northdene Rd. LE2—5G 15
Northdown Dri. LE4—3G 5
North Dri. LE5—2D 10
N. End Clo. LE2—4F 15
Northfield Av. LE4—1D 4
Northfield Av. LE8—1H 21
  (in two parts)
Northfield Rd. LE8—1B 10
Northfield Rd. LE8—3C 20
Northfields. LE7—4B 28
Northfold Rd. LE2—4A 16
Northgate St. LE3—3E 9
North Rd. LE11—1G 27
North St. LE2—5D 16
North St. LE7—5A 28

North St. LE8—1B 22
Northumberland Av. LE4—6E 5
Northumberland Rd. LE8
       —1F 21
Northumberland St. LE1—3F 9
Norton St. LE1—5F 9
Norwich Rd. LE4—5A 4
Norwood Rd. LE5—6C 10
Nottingham Rd. LE5—4B 10
Nottingham Rd. LE11—2G 27
Nugent St. LE3—3D 8
Nursery Clo. LE2—2F 5
Nursery Clo. LE7—3D 28
Nursery Clo. LE9—2A 18
Nursery Hollow. LE2—1C 20
Nursery Rd. LE3—3G 11
Nutfield Rd. LE3—6D 8
Nuthall Gro. LE2—6C 14

Oadby Hill Dri. LE2—4D 16
Oadby Rd. LE8—1B 22
Oak Cres. LE3—1G 13
Oakcroft Av. LE9—4C 6
Oakdene Rd. LE2—5G 15
Oak Dri. LE7—6A 28
Oakenshaw Clo. LE4—3B 4
Oakfield Av. LE3—6D 2
Oakfield Av. LE4—1B 4
Oakfield Cres. LE8—5D 20
Oakfield Rd. LE2—6A 10
Oakham Clo. LE11—3B 26
Oakhurst Ct. LE11—3B 26
Oakland Av. LE4—4D 4
Oakland Rd. LE2—2G 15
Oaklands Av. LE11—4E 27
Oakleigh Av. LE2—3F 21
Oakley Rd. LE5—3B 10
Oak Pool Gdns. LE2—1E 21
Oak Rd. LE9—6G 19
Oaks Dri. LE5—5D 20
Oakside Clo. LE4—1D 4
Oakside Cres. LE5—5F 11
Oaks Industrial Est. LE9—5E 19
Oak St. LE5—2A 10
Oaks Way. LE2—2D 16
Oakthorpe Av. LE3—5C 8
Oaktree Clo. LE6—3B 2
Oakwood Av. LE8—6B 16
Oban St. LE3—3D 8
Ocean Clo. LE5—3F 11
Ocean Rd. LE5—3F 11
Odam Clo. LE3—1B 14
Offranville Clo. LE4—2G 5
Ogwen Clo. LE5—4G 11
Okehampton Av. LE5—6C 10
Okehampton Wlk. LE5—6C 10
Old Ashby Rd. LE11—5A 26
Old Barn Wlk. LE4—5F 3
Old Church St. LE2—4D 14
Old Mill La. LE1—3G 9
Old Milton St. LE1—3G 9
Old Saffron La. LE2—2F 15
Oliver Rd. LE4—6D 4
Oliver Rd. LE11—4F 27
Oliver St. LE2—2F 15
Olphin St. LE4—1G 9
Olympic Clo. LE3—1H 7
Onslow St. LE2—5A 10
Ontario Clo. LE1—2G 9
Orange St. LE8—4F 21
Orchard Av. LE2—2C 20
Orchard Clo. LE2—6E 17
Orchard Dri. LE8—2H 21
Orchard La. LE8—2H 25
Orchard Rd. LE4—1D 4
Orchardson Av. LE4—2H 9
Orchard St. LE1—3G 9
Orchard St. LE11—3F 27
Orchard, The. LE8—3A 2
Oriel Dri. LE7—6B 28
Oriel Ho. LE5—4D 10
Orkney Way. LE8—2H 25
Orlando Rd. LE7—1H 15
Orme Clo. LE4—5F 3
Ormen Grn. LE3—3H 7
Oronsay Rd. LE4—5G 3
Orson Dri. LE8—1H 21
Orson St. LE5—4B 10
Orton Rd. LE4—5B 4
Orwell Clo. LE11—1C 26
Osborne Rd. LE5—4B 10
Osborne St. LE11—1C 26

Osiers, The. LE3—4A 14
Osmaston Rd. LE5—5A 10
Osterley Clo. LE11—2C 26
Ottawa Rd. LE1—3G 9
Outwood Clo. LE3—4H 7
Outwoods Av. LE11—4F 9
Outwoods Dri. LE11—5D 26
Oval, The. LE1—5H 9
Overdale Av. LE3—5B 2
Overdale Clo. LE3—6B 2
Overdale Rd. LE4—4H 15
Overdale Rd. LE4—2G 5
Overfield Clo. LE6—1C 6
Overfield Wlk. LE6—1C 6
Overing Clo. LE5—5C 4
Overpark Av. LE3—5B 8
Overseal Rd. LE2—2A 8
Overton Rd. LE5—2B 10
Owen Clo. LE4—3G 5
Owston Dri. LE8—1H 21
Oxburgh Clo. LE11—3C 26
Oxendon St. LE2—4H 9
Oxford Av. LE2—6H 9
Oxford Dri. LE8—2F 21
Oxford Rd. LE2—1H 15
Oxford St. LE1—5F 9
Oxford St. LE7—5B 28
Oxford St. LE11—2E 27
Oxon Way. LE4—4D 10
Oxted Rise. LE2—1D 22

Packer Av. LE3—5F 7
Packe St. LE11—3F 27
Packhorse Grn. LE2—1E 21
Packhorse La. LE11—3F 27
Packhorse Rd. LE2—1E 21
Packman Grn. LE8—2H 25
Packwood Rd. LE4—4A 4
Paddock Clo. LE2—5C 16
Paddock Clo. LE8—2H 25
Paddock Clo. LE8—2B 22
Padstow Rd. LE4—5G 5
Paget Av. LE4—1D 4
Paget Rd. LE3—3D 8
Paget St. LE2—5D 14
Paget St. LE11—2E 27
Paigle Rd. LE2—4D 14
Painter St. LE1—2G 9
Palmer Av. LE11—1E 27
Palmerston Boulevd. LE2
       —5A 16
Palmer St. LE4—5C 4
Pamela Pl. LE4—4A 4
Pantain Rd. LE11—6D 26
Parade, The. LE2—5D 16
Paradise La. LE3—3F 9
Pares St. LE1—4F 9
Park Av. LE2—3F 15
Park Av. LE11—5F 27
Park Clo. LE3—3B 24
Park Ct. LE11—4F 27
Park Cres. LE2—1F 23
Parkdale Rd. LE4—2G 5
Park Dri. LE3—2F 7
  (Glenfield)
Park Dri. LE3—6G 7
  (Leicester Forest E.)
Parker Dri. LE4—6A 4
Park Hill Dri. LE2—3E 15
Park Hill Dri. LE2—3E 15
Parkland Dri. LE2—4D 16
Parklands Av. LE6—2A 2
Parklands Dri. LE11—6E 27
  (in two parts)
Park Rise. LE3—4H 7
Park Rd. LE4—2B 4
Park Rd. LE6—2B 6
Park Rd. LE7—3D 2
Park Rd. LE8—4C 20
  (Blaby)
Park Rd. LE8—4F 21
  (Wigston)
Park Rd. LE9—3B 24
Parkside. LE2—3E 15
Parkside Clo. LE8—4A 22
Parkstone Rd. LE5—2G 11
Parkstone Rd. LE7—4E 28
Park St. LE1—5G 9

36

Park St. LE11—4F 27
Park Vale Rd. LE5—4A 10
Park View. LE3—4H 7
Parkway, The. LE5—3E 11
Parliament St. LE2—6F 9
Parry St. LE5—3A 10
Parsons Dri. LE2—1C 20
Parvian Rd. LE2—6G 15
Pasley Clo. LE2—1E 21
Pasley Rd. LE2—6E 15
Pasture La. LE1—3F 9
Paton St. LE3—5E 9
Patterdale Dri. LE11—6C 26
Patterdale Rd. LE4—2G 5
Paul Dri. LE4—4H 5
Pauline Av. LE4—4D 4
Pawley Gdns. LE2—6D 14
Pawley Grn. LE2—6D 14
Payne St. LE4—5D 4
Peacock La. LE1—4F 9
Peake Rd. LE4—1B 10
Peartree Clo. LE7—3D 2
Pear Tree La. LE11—1A 26
Peatling Rd. LE8—2H 25
Pedlars Clo. LE4—5G 3
Pedlars Way. LE7—2C 28
Peebles Way. LE4—5F 5
Peel Dri. LE11—2G 27
Peewit Clo. LE2—1C 20
Pegasus Clo. LE2—4H 9
Pelham St. LE1—5F 9
Pelham St. LE2—4D 16
Pembroke Av. LE7—6B 28
Pembroke Av. LE8—2F 21
Pembroke St. LE5—2A 10
Pen Clo. LE2—6F 15
Pendene Rd. LE2—2A 16
Pendlebury Dri. LE2—4H 15
Penfold Dri. LE8—2G 25
Penhale Rd. LE3—3A 14
Penkridge Wlk. LE4—4B 4
Pennant Clo. LE3—3H 7
Pennine Clo. LE2—6G 17
Penny Clo. LE8—1A 22
Penny Long La. LE3—6E 7
Penrith Rd. LE4—6E 5
Penryn Dri. LE8—3A 22
Pensilva Clo. LE8—3A 22
Pentonville. LE2—5F 9
Pentridge Clo. LE8—4A 22
Penzance Av. LE8—3A 22
Peppercorn Clo. LE4—5H 3
Percival St. LE5—3A 10
Percy Rd. LE2—4F 15
Percy St. LE3—3C 14
Perkyn Rd. LE5—3F 11
Perseverance Rd. LE4—3C 4
Perth Av. LE3—2B & 3B 8
Peters Dri. LE5—2E 11
Petersfield. LE9—6A 24
Petworth Dri. LE3—3C 8
Petworth Dri. LE11—2B 26
Pevensey Av. LE5—6G 11
Pevensey Rd. LE11—1D 26
Peverel Ct. LE3—2A 14
Peverel Rd. LE3—1C 14
Phoenix Clo. LE3—2C 8
Piccaver Rise. LE3—4H 7
Pickwell Clo. LE3—2A 8
Piers Rd. LE3—1G 7
Pike St. LE1—3G 9
Pilgrim Gdns. LE5—6D 10
Pilkington Rd. LE3—6A 8
Pindar Rd. LE3—2B 8
Pine Dri. LE7—6A 28
Pine Rd. LE3—2G 7
Pine Tree Av. LE5—2D 10
Pine Tree Clo. LE2—1E 23
Pine Tree Clo. LE3—1D 12
Pinewood Av. LE4—3F 5
Pinewood Clo. LE8—1H 25
Pinfold. LE3—4A 14
Pinfold Ga. LE11—3G 27
Pinfold Jetty. LE11—3G 27
Pinfold Rd. LE4—2E 5
Pingle St. LE3—3E 9
Piper Clo. LE3—2B 8
Piper Way. LE3—2B 8
Pipe Wlk. LE4—5B 4
Pitchens Clo. LE4—3E 3
Pits Av. LE3—4A 14
Pitsford Dri. LE11—4A 26
Pitton Clo. LE8—4A 22
Plantation Av. LE2—5D 14
Plantation, The. LE8—2H 25
Player Clo. LE4—3F 5
Ploughmans' Lea. LE7—2C 28
Plowman Clo. LE3—1G 7
Plumtree Way. LE7—6B 28
Pluto Clo. LE2—4H 9
Plymouth Dri. LE5—6C 10
Plymstock Clo. LE3—3C 8
Pochins Clo. LE8—2A 22
Pochin St. LE9—6A 24
Pocklingtons Wlk. LE1—4F 9
Polaris Clo. LE2—4H 9
Pollard Rd. LE3—6A 8
Pomeroy Dri. LE2—5C 16
Pool Rd. LE3—3C 8
Pope Cres. LE9—1E 19
Pope St. LE2—3G 15
Poplar Av. LE4—1C 4
Poplar Av. LE8—2G 25
Poplar Rd. LE9—6F 19
Poplar Rd. LE11—6F 27
Poplars Clo. LE6—2A 2
Poplar Ter. LE7—2D 2
Porlock St. LE3—4C 8
Portcullis Rd. LE5—1H 11
Portishead Rd. LE5—1B 10
Portland Rd. LE2—1A 16
Portland Rd. LE9—5D 6
Portland St. LE9—2B 24
Portland Towers. LE2—3C 16
Portland Wlk. LE2—1F 23
Portloc Dri. LE8—3A 22
Portman St. LE4—6D 4
Portmore Clo. LE4—5H 3
Portsdown Rd. LE2—4B 16
Portsmouth Rd. LE4—6D 4
Portwey, The. LE5—2C 10
Post Office La. LE8—5G 23
Potter St. LE1—3G 9
Potterton Rd. LE4—4A 4
Powys Av. LE2—2C 16
Poynings Av. LE3—3B 8
Prebend St. LE2—5H 9
Prestbury Rd. LE11—2B 26
Prestwold Rd. LE5—2A 10
Pretoria Rd. LE9—4C 6
Primrose Hill. LE2—5D 16
Prince Albert Dri. LE3—2G 7
Prince Dri. LE2—6F 17
Princes Clo. LE7—2D 2
Princess Av. LE2—6F 17
Princess Dri. LE9—5C 6
Princess Rd. E. LE1—5G 9
Princess Rd. W. LE1—5G 9
Princess St. LE9—4G 19
Princess St. LE11—4F 27
Priory Cres. LE3—4A 8
Priory Rd. LE11—6D 26
Priory Wlk. LE3—6E 7
Progress Way. LE4—5H 5
Prospect Hill. LE5—3A 10
Prospect Rd. LE5—3A 10
Pulford Dri. LE7—3H 11
Pullman Rd. LE8—2H 21
Pulteney Av. LE11—6G 27
Pulteney Rd. LE11—6F 27
Purbeck Clo. LE8—4B 22
Purcell Rd. LE4—1G 9
Purley Rd. LE4—6E 5
Putney Rd. W. LE2—1F 15
Pymn Ley. La. LE6—3B & 5A 2
Pytchley Clo. LE4—4B 4
Pytchley Dri. LE11—6E 27

Quarry La. LE9—6F 13
Quebec Rd. LE1—3H 9
Queens Dri. LE3—6E 7
Queens Dri. LE8—2H 21
Queens Dri. LE9—2H 19
Queensferry Pde. LE2—1D 20
Queensgate Dri. LE4—1B 4
Queens Pk. Way. LE2—2E 21
(in two parts)
Queens Rd. LE2—1H to 3H 15
Queen's Rd. LE8—4C 20
Queen's Rd. LE11—2G 27
Queen St. LE1—4G 9
Queen St. LE2—5E 17
Queen St. LE11—3G 27
Quenby St. LE5—2B 10
Queniborough Rd. LE4—1A 10
Queniborough Rd. LE7—3D 28
(Queniborough)
Queniborough Rd. LE7—6C 28
(Syston)
Quiney Way. LE2—4F 17
Quinton Rise. LE2—6E 17
Quorn Av. LE2—6F 17
Quorn Clo. LE11—5H 27
Quorn Rd. LE5—2B 10

Radcot Lawns. LE2—1E 21
Radford Dri. LE3—6G 7
Radiant Rd. LE5—2F 11
Radmoor Rd. LE11—3E 27
Radnor Rd. LE8—1G 21
Radstone Wlk. LE5—4D 10
Raeburn Rd. LE2—2H 15
Ragdale Rd. LE4—1A 10
Railway St. LE8—4F 21
Railway Ter. LE11—1H 27
Rainsford Cres. LE4—5B 4
Ramsbury Rd. LE2—5H 15
Ramsdean Av. LE8—1A 22
Ramsey Gdns. LE5—1H 11
Ramsey Way. LE5—1G 11
Rancliffe Cres. LE3—5B 8
Rannoch Clo. LE4—5H 3
Ranton Way. LE3—1D 8
Ranworth Wlk. LE4—4B 4
Ratby La. LE9 & LE3—3D 6 to 5G 7
Ratby Meadow La. LE9—1A 20
Ratby Rd. LE6—3A 2
Ratcliffe. LE2—3A 16
Ratcliffe Ct. LE2—2B 16
Ratcliffe Dri. LE9—5C 18
Ratcliffe Rd. LE2—3A 16
Ratcliffe Rd. LE11—1G 27
Ratcliffe St. LE4—6D 4
Ravenhurst Rd. LE3—2B 14
Raven Rd. LE3—6A 8
Ravensbridge Dri. LE4—1E 9
Ravensthorpe Dri. LE11—4A 26
Ravensthorpe Rd. LE8—2B 22
Raw Dykes Rd. LE2—1F 15
Rawlings Pas. LE2—5D 16
Rawlinson Wlk. LE4—5H 3
Rawson St. LE1—5G 9
Rawson St. LE9—1F 19
Rawstone Wlk. LE4—1H 9
Rayleigh Grn. LE5—1G 11
Rayleigh Way. LE5—1H 11
Raymond Av. LE11—1C 26
Raymond Rd. LE3—6D 8
Raynham Dri. LE11—2C 26
Reading St. LE4—3E 5
Rearsby Rd. LE4—6E 5
Rearsby Rd. LE7—3D 28
Rectory Clo. LE8—3A 22
Rectory Gdns. LE2—1E 17
Rectory Pl. LE11—2F 27
Rectory Rd. LE11—2G 27
Redcar Rd. LE4—6D 4
Red Hill. LE4—3C 4
Red Hill Av. LE9—4F 19
Red Hill Circle. LE4—4C 4
Red Hill Clo. LE4—1G 5
Red Hill La. LE4—1G 5
(in two parts)
Red Ho. Clo. LE2—1D 20
Red Ho. Gdns. LE2—1D 20
Red Ho. Rise. LE2—1D 20
Red Ho. Rd. LE2—1D 20
Redmarle Rd. LE3—6B 8
Redmires Clo. LE11—4B 26
Redpath Clo. LE4—2H 9
Redruth Av. LE8—3A 22
Redwing Ct. LE5—3A 10
Redwood Wlk. LE5—2A 10
Reed Pool Clo. LE8—2H 25
Rees Gro. LE4—3F 5
Reeth Clo. LE4—5H 3
Regent Clo. LE8—2H 21
Regent Rd. LE1—5G 9
Regent Rd. LE8—1H 25
Regent St. LE1—5G 9
Regent St. LE2—4D 16
Regent St. LE9—4G 19
Regent St. LE11—2E 27
Regent Wlk. LE3—6E 7
Rendell Rd. LE4—1H 9
Rendell St. LE11—1F & 1G 27
Renfrew Rd. LE5—1G 11
Renishaw Dri. LE5—1C 16
Repington Row. LE2—5F 15
Repton Rd. LE8—6H 15
Repton St. LE3—3E 9
Retreat, The. LE5—5C 10
Reynolds Pl. LE3—1B 14
Ribble Av. LE2—4F 17
Richard Clo. LE3—6G 7
Richard III Rd. LE3—4E 9
Richmond Av. LE2—2F 15
Richmond Clo .LE2—2F 15
Ricmond Clo. LE9—3A 24
Ricmond Dri. LE2—3E 21
Richmond Rd. LE2—2F 15
Richmond St. LE2—5F 9
Richmond Way. LE2—1F 23
Riddington Rd. LE3—4B 14
Riddington Rd. LE9—6G 19
Ridgemere La. LE7—5D 28
Ridgeway. LE2—1E 23
Ridgeway. LE9—6G 19
Ridgeway Dri. LE4—2H 5
Ridgeway Rd. LE2—3B 16
Ridings, The. LE7—4D 28
Ridley Clo. LE8—6B 20
Ridley St. LE3—5E 9
Ringers Clo. LE2—3D 16
Ringers Spinney. LE2—2E 17
Ring Rd. LE2—4A & 4B 16
Ringway, The. LE7—3D 28
Ringwood Clo. LE8—3A 22
Ringwood Rd. LE5—1G 11
Ripon Dri. LE8—6C 20
Ripon St. LE2—6A 10
Riston Clo. LE2—1E 23
Riverside Clo. LE4—2D 4
Rivers St. LE3—4E 9
Rivington Dri. LE11—4B 26
Robert Hall St. LE4—5C 4
Robertsbridge Av. LE4—5B 4
Robertsbridge Wlk. LE4—5B 4
Roberts Rd. LE4—1G 9
Robin Clo. LE2—4F 15
Robinson Rd. LE5—3C 10
Roborough Grn. LE5—3H 11
Robotham Clo. LE9—4C 18
Roche Clo. LE2—1D 20
Rockingham Clo. LE5—4E 11
Rockingham Clo. LE8—5C 20
Rockingham Rd. LE11—1D 26
Rockley Rd. LE4—1D 8
Roehampton Dri. LE8—5H 15
Rogerstone Rd. LE5—5G 11
Rolleston Rd. LE8—1H 21
Rolleston Sq. LE5—4B 10
Rolleston St. LE5—3B 10
Roman Rd. LE4—3C 4
Roman St. LE3—5E 9
Romway Av. LE5—1C 16
Romway Rd. LE5—1B 16
Rona Gdns. LE5—3H 11
Rookery La. LE4—2F 5
Rookery La. LE6—2B & 5A 2
Rookery, The. LE6—2B 2
Rosamund Av. LE3—3B 14
Rosebank Rd. LE8—2H 25
Rosebarn Way. LE5—1F 11
Rosebery Rd. LE7—2D 2
Rosebery St. LE5—4B 10
Rosebery St. LE11—2E 27
Rosedale Av. LE4—6E 5
Rosedale Rd. LE8—2D 22
Rosedene Av. LE4—3F 5
Rose Farm Clo. LE3—5B 8
Rosehill. LE11—2B 26
Rosemead Dri. LE2—6D 16
Rosedene Clo. LE9—5E 7
Roseneath Av. LE4—5F 5
Rose St. LE4—6C 4
Rose Tree Av. LE4—1C 4
Roseway. LE4—5F 5
Roslyn St. LE2—5A 10
Rossett Dri. LE4—6A 4
Rosshill Cres. LE5—2G 11
Ross's La. LE8—2B 22
Ross Wlk. LE4—1G 9
(in two parts)
Rotherby Av. LE4—1A 10
Rothley St. LE4—1H 9
Roughton St. LE4—5D 4
Roundhay Rd. LE3—1D 14
Roundhill Clo. LE7—6A 28
Roundhill Rd. LE5—6B 10
Roundway, The. LE4—3H 5
Rowanberry Av. LE3—3G 7
Rowans, The. LE8—1G 25
Rowan St. LE3—3D 8
Rowlands Way. LE2—2C 20
Rowlatts Hill Rd. LE5—4D 10
Rowley Fields Av. LE3—2C 14
Rowsley Av. LE5—5B 10
Rowsley St. LE5—6A 10
Royal E. St. LE1—3G 9
Royal Rd. LE4—6D 4
Royal Way. LE11—1E 27
Royce Hall. LE11—4C 26
Roy Clo. LE9—4G 19
Roydale Clo. LE11—1D 26
Roydene Cres. LE4—6H 3
Royland Rd. LE11—4F 27
Royston Clo. LE2—2D 20
Ruby St. LE3—3D 8
Ruddington Wlk. LE4—4B 4
Ruding Rd. LE3—5E 9
Ruding St. LE3—4E 9
Rudyard Clo. LE11—4B 26
Rufford St. LE5—4C 10
Rugby St. LE3—2E 9
Runcorn Clo. LE2—1D 20
Runcorn Rd. LE2—1D 20
Rupert Brooke Rd. LE11—2C 26
Rupert St. LE1—4F 9
Rushes, The. LE11—2F 27
Rushey Clo. LE4—4E 5
Rushford Clo. LE4—1B 10
Rushford Dri. LE4—1B 10
Rushmere Wlk. LE3—1E 13
Rushton Dri. LE2—6C 14
Ruskin Av. LE7—6B 28
Ruskington Dri. LE8—6B 16
Russell Sq. LE1—2G 9
Russell St. LE11—3G 27
Rutherford Hall. LE11—4C 26
Rutland Av. LE2—2E 15
Rutland Av. LE8—1H 21
Rutland Clo. LE3—6E 7
Rutland Dri. LE4—2F 5
Rutland Hall. LE11—3D 26
Rutland St. LE1—4G 9
Rutland St. LE11—3G 27
Rydal Av. LE11—5C 26
Rydal Ho. LE2—1D 20
Rydal St. LE2—5F 9
Ryde Av. LE2—4B 16
Rye Clo. LE2—1E 21
Ryegate Cres. LE4—1C 4

Sacheverel Rd. LE3—3H 7
Sackville Gdns. LE2—3A 16
Saddlers' Clo. LE7—2C 28
Saffron Hill Rd. LE2—3F 15
Saffron La. LE2—1F to 6F 15
Saffron Rd. LE8—1F 21
Saffron Way. LE2—4E 15
St. Albans Rd. LE2—5H 9
St. Andrew's Dri. LE2—2C 16
St. Andrew's Rd. LE2—4F 15
St. Anne's Dri. LE2—4D 14
St. Augustine Rd. LE3—4E 9
St. Austell Rd. LE5—2G 11
St. Barnabas Rd. LE5—3B 10
St. Bernard's Av. LE4—5D 4
St. Bernard St. LE4—5D 4
Saintbury Rd. LE3—6C 2
St. David's Cres. LE2—2C 16
St. Denys Rd. LE5—5E 11
St. Dunstan's Rd. LE3—4D 8
St. George St. LE1—4G 9
(in two parts)
St. George's Way. LE1—4H 9
St. Helen's Clo. LE4—1D 8
St. Helen's Dri. LE4—1D 8
St. Ives Rd. LE4—5G 5
St. Ives Rd. LE8—3A 22
St. James Clo. LE2—1F 23
St. James Clo. LE9—5C 18
St. James Rd. LE2—6A 10
St. James St. LE1—3G 9
St. James Ter. LE2—6A 10
St. Johns. LE9—2H 19
St. John's Av. LE7—6B 28
St. John's Rd. LE2—1A 16
St. John St. LE1—3F 9
St. Leonard's Ct. LE2—1H 15
St. Leonard's Rd. LE2—1H & 2H 15
St. Luke's Clo. LE7—5H 11
St. Margaret's St. LE1—3F 9
St. Margaret's Way. LE1 & LE4—2F 9
St. Mark's St. LE1—2G 9
St. Martin's. LE1—4F 9
St. Martin's E. LE1—4F 9
St. Martin's W. LE1—4F 9
St. Mary's Av. LE3—6G 7
St. Mary's Av. LE5—2F 11
St. Mary's Rd. LE2—1H 15
St. Matthew's Way. LE1—3G 9
St. Michael's Av. LE4—5D 4
St. Michael's Ct. LE4—1F 5
St. Nicholas Circle. LE1—4F 9
St. Nicholas Pl. LE1—4F 9
St. Oswald's Rd. LE3—2A 8
St. Paul's Dri. LE7—6A 28
St. Paul's Rd. LE3—4D 8
St. Peter's Clo. LE3—1F 7
St. Peter's Dri. LE8—4B 20
St. Peter's Path. LE2—5D 16
St. Peter's La. LE1—3F 9
St. Peter's Rd. LE2—5H 9
St. Peter's St. LE7—5A 28
St. Philip's Rd. LE5—6B 10
St. Saviour's Hill. LE5—3A 10
St. Saviour's Rd. LE5—3A to 4C 10
St. Stephen's Rd. LE2—5A 10
St. Swithin's Rd. LE5—4G 11
St. Thomas Rd. LE8—3F 21
St. Wolstan's Clo. LE8—1B 22
Salcombe Dri. LE3—1G 7
Salisbury Av. LE1—5H 9
Salisbury Av. LE9—6A 24
Salisbury Clo. LE8—6C 20
Salisbury Rd. LE1—6H 9
Salisbury St. LE11—2G 27
Salkeld Rd. LE2—2D 20
Saltash Clo. LE8—3A 22
Saltcoats Av. LE4—4E 5
Saltersford Rd. LE5—3C 10
Saltersgate Dri. LE4—1C 4
Samson Rd. LE3—2C 8
Samuel St. LE1—4H 9
Sandacre St. LE1—3F 9
Sandalwood Rd. LE11—5D 26
Sandfield Clo. LE4—3F 5
Sandford Clo. LE5—4D 10
Sandford Rd. LE7—6A 28
Sandgate Av. LE4—1C 4
Sandhill Dri. LE9—3G 19
Sandhurst Clo. LE3—3C 8
Sandhurst Rd. LE3—3C 8
Sandhurst St. LE2—5D 16
Sandiacre Dri. LE4—1G 5
Sandown Rd. LE2—1B 16
Sandown Rd. LE3—1G 7
Sandown Rd. LE8—6B 16
Sandpiper Clo. LE5—3A 10
Sandringham Av. LE4—5D 4
Sandringham Dri. LE11—2C 26
Sandringham Rd. LE2—3E 21
Sandy Rise. LE8—1C 22
Sanvey Clo. LE2—4D 14
Sanvey Ga. LE1—3F 9
Sanvey La. LE2—4C 14
Sarah St. LE3—4E 9
Saunderson Rd. LE4—4A 4
Savernake Rd. LE4—6H 3
Saville Rd. LE8—5D 20
Saville St. LE5—4C 10
Sawday St. LE2—6F 9
Sawley St. LE5—6A 10
Saxby St. LE2—5H 9
Saxon Dale. LE2—2D 20
Saxons Rise. LE6—1B 6
Saxon St. LE3—5E 9
Scalpay Clo. LE4—5G 3
Scarborough Rd. LE4—6E 5
Schaeffer Ct. LE4—5G 3
Schofield Rd. LE11—4C 26
School Clo. LE9—6A 24
Schoolgate. LE2—6G 15
School La. LE4—2C 4
School La. LE5—1E 17

School La. LE9—4C 18
(Huncote)
School La. LE9—4G 19
(Narborough)
School St. LE7—5A 28
School St. LE11—3G 27
Scotland Way. LE8—2H 25
Scotswood Cres. LE2—1D 20
Scott St. LE2—3G 15
Scraptoft La. LE5—2D 10 to 2H 11
Scraptoft Rise. LE7—2H 11
Scudamore Rd. LE3—4F 7
Seaford Rd. LE2—5E 15
Seagrave Dri. LE2—5C 16
Seaton Rise. LE5—1G 11
Seaton Rd. LE8—3A 22
Seddons Clo. LE4—4A 4
Sedgebrook Clo. LE5—5G 11
Sedgebrook Rd. LE5—5G 11
Sedgefield Dri. LE7—4H 11
Segrave Rd. LE3—1C 14
Seine La. LE9—1D 18
Selbourne St. LE11—3G 27
Selbury Dri. LE2—5C 16
Selby Av. LE5—1G 11
Selkirk Rd. LE4—4F 5
Seton Clo. LE11—1C 26
Severn Clo. LE9—2B 24
Severn Rd. LE2—5F 17
Severn St. LE2—5H 9
Seward St. LE11—3E 27
Sextant Rd. LE5—2F 11
Seymour Rd. LE2—1H 15
Seymour St. LE2—5H 9
Shackerdale Rd. LE8 & LE2 —6H 15
Shackleton St. LE1—2G 9
Shady La. LE2—2E 17
Shaftesbury Av. LE4—6D 4
Shaftesbury Rd. LE3—5D 8
Shakespeare Clo. LE3—2A 14
Shakespeare Dri. LE3—2A 14
Shakespeare St. LE2—2F 15
Shakespeare St. LE11—2F 27
Shanklin Av. LE2—4B 16
Shanklin Dri. LE2—4A 16
Shanklin Gdns. LE2—4B 16
Shanklin Gdns. LE3—1F 13
Shardlow Rd. LE8—1A 22
Sharmon Cres. LE3—4H 7
Sharpland. LE2—6D 14
Sharpley Rd. LE11—4B 26
Shaw Wood Clo. LE6—2A 2
Shearer Clo. LE4—4G 5
Shearsby Clo. LE8—2B 22
Sheene Rd. LE4—4F 3
Sheepwash La. LE7—2E 3
Sheffield St. LE3—6E 9
Shelbourne St. LE5—4A 10
Sheldon St. LE5—3H 9
Shelford Wlk. LE4—5B 4
Shelley Rd. LE9—2E 19
Shelley St. LE2—3H 15
Shelley St. LE11—2C 26
Shelthorpe Av. LE11—5G 27
Shelthorpe Rd. LE11—5G 27
Shenley Rd. LE8—6C 16
Shenton Clo. LE8—1A 22
Shepherds Clo. LE3—6C 6
Shepherds Clo. LE11—5C 26
Shepherd's Wlk. LE7—2C 28
Sherborne Av. LE8—4A 22
Sherford Clo. LE8—2A 22
Sheridan Clo. LE9—2E 19
Sheridan St. LE2—2F 15
Sheringham Rd. LE4—6A 4
Sherrard Rd. LE5—3A 10
Sherwood St. LE5—4C 10
Shetland Rd. LE4—6E 5
Shetland Way. LE8—2H 25
Shield Cres. LE2—2D 20
Shipley Rd. LE5—5A 10
Shipston Hill. LE2—6D 16
Shipton Clo. LE8—2C 22
Shire Clo. LE3—4H 7
Shirley Av. LE2—3B 16
Shirley Dri. LE7—4B 28
Shirley Rd. LE2—3B 16
Shirley St. LE4—6C 4
Shortridge La. LE9—2F 19
Short St. LE1—3F 9
Shottens Clo. LE4—6G 3
Shottery Av. LE3—2A 14
Shrewsbury Av. LE2—5G 15
Shropshire Rd. LE2—4E 15
Shuttleworth La. LE9—4A & 6C 24
Sibson Rd. LE4—1C 4
Sibton La. LE2—6D 16
Sickleholm Dri. LE5—1C 16
Sidmouth Av. LE5—6D 10
Sidney Rd. LE2—3B 16
Sidwell St. LE5—4B 10
Silbury Rd. LE4—1D 8
Silsden Rise. LE2—2E 21
Silver Birch Way. LE7—1D 28
Silverdale Dri. LE4—2G 5
Silverstone Dri. LE4—3F 5
Silver St. LE1—4F 9
Silverton Clo. LE2—5F 17
Silverton Rd. LE11—6E 27
Silverwood Clo. LE5—4F 11
Simmins Clo. LE2—1D 20
Simmins Cres. LE2—1E 21
Sir Robert Martin Ct. LE11 —1C 26
Siskin Hill. LE2—6D 16
Sitwell Wlk. LE5—1C 16
Skampton Grn. LE5—4E 11
Skampton Rd. LE5—5E 11
Skelton Dri. LE2—5G 15
Sketchley Clo. LE5—3G 11
Skipworth St. LE2—5A 10
Skye Way. LE8—2H 25
Slade Greens, The. LE2—6D 14
Slade Pl. LE2—6D 14
Slater St. LE3—2E 9
Slate St. LE2—4H 9
Sloane Clo. LE9—1F 19
Smedmore Rd. LE5—2B 10
Smith Av. LE4—3H 5
Smith Dorrien Rd. LE5—3B 10
Snell's Nook La. LE12—5A 26
Snow Hill. LE4—1D 8
Soar La. LE3—3E 9
Somerby Dri. LE2—5F 17
Somerby Rd. LE7—3H 11
Somerfield Wlk. LE4—5G 3
Somerset Av. LE4—6A 4
Somers Rd. LE5—3F 11
Somerville Rd. LE3—2C 14
Sonning Way. LE2—2D 20
Sopers Rd. LE9—6A 24
S. Albion St. LE1—5G 9
Southampton St. LE1—4G 9
South Av. LE3—6F 7
South Av. LE8—2A 22
S. Bond St. LE1—4F 9
S. Church Ga. LE1—3F 9
Southdown Dri. LE4—3F 5
Southdown Rd. LE5—3B 10
Southdown Rd. LE11—6E 27
South Dri. LE5—2D 10
Southernhay Av. LE2—2A 16
Southernhay Clo. LE2—2A 16
Southernhay Rd. LE2—2A 16
Southey Clo. LE4—2H 9
Southey Clo. LE9—2E 19
Southfield Av. LE7—6B 28
Southfield Clo. LE2—1B 20
Southfield Rd. LE11—3F 27
Southfields Av. LE2—4C 16
Southfields Dri. LE2—5F 15
Southgates. LE1—4F 9
Southgates Underpass. LE1 —4F 9
S. Kingsmead Rd. LE2—5A 16
S. Knighton Rd. LE2—3B 16
Southland Rd. LE2—4B 16
Southmeads Clo. LE2—3D 16
Southmeads Rd. LE2—3D 16
South St. LE2—5D 16
South St. LE11—3F 27
Southview Dri. LE5—1C 16
South Wlk. LE6—1B 6
Southway. LE8—5C 20
Spa La. LE8—2B 22
Spalding St. LE5—3B 10
Sparkenhoe. LE9—6A 24
Sparkenhoe St. LE2—4H 9
Sparrow Hill. LE11—2G 27
Speers Rd. LE3—2A 8
Spencefield Dri. LE5—6E 11
Spencefield La. LE5—6E 11
Spencer Av. LE4—2F 5
Spencer St. LE2—4D 16
Spence St. LE5—3B 10
Spendlow Gdns. LE2—6E 15
Spendlow Grn. LE2—6F 15
Spinney Av. LE8—1H 25
Spinney Clo. LE2—1B 20
Spinney Hill Dri. LE11—5C 26
Spinney Hill Rd. LE5—3A 10
Spinney Rise. LE4—1C 4
Spinneyside. LE6—3B 2
Sponne Rise. LE2—6F 15
Sportsfield La. LE9—4C 18
Sports Rd. LE3—1G 7
Springbrook Dri. LE7—3H 11
Spring Clo. LE2—6D 14
Springdale Rd. LE4—2G 5
Springfield Clo. LE11—6D 26
Springfield Rd. LE2—1A 16
Spring Gdns. LE9—5G 19
Spring La. LE8—1B 22
Springway Clo. LE5—4G 11
Springwell Clo. LE8—2G 25
Springwell Dri. LE8—2G 25
Springwell La. LE8—1C 24
Square, The. LE3—1F 7
Square, The. LE8—2H 25
(Countesthorpe)
Square, The. LE8—5G 23
(Newton Harcourt)
Square, The. LE9—5G 19
Squire's Ride. LE7—1C 28
Squirrel's Corner. LE7—1D 28
Stadium Pl. LE4—6A 4
Stadon Rd. LE7—2D 2
Stafford Dri. LE8—2G 21
Stafford Leys. LE3—6E 7
Stafford St. LE4—5E 5
Staindale. LE8—2C 22
Stamford Clo. LE3—1G 7
Stamford Hall. LE2—3D 16
Stamford Rd. LE9—5D 6
Stamford St. LE1—4G 9
Stamford St. LE3—1F 7
Stamford St. LE6—1B 6
Stancliff Rd. LE4—3G 5
Stanfell Rd. LE2—2H 15
Stanhope Rd. LE8—3C 22
Stanhope St. LE5—4B 10
Stanley Dri. LE5—2E 11
Stanley Rd. LE2—6A 10
Stanley St. LE11—4F 27
Stanton La. LE9—6A 18
Stanton Row. LE2—5G 15
Stanyon Clo. LE8—2H 25
Stapleford Rd. LE4—4A 4
Staplehurst Av. LE3—3A 14
Station Av. LE11—2E 27
Station Clo. LE9—5C 6
Station Dri. LE9—5D 6
Station La. LE7—3H 11
Station Rd. LE3—1G 7
Station Rd. LE4—3B 4
Station Rd. LE6—2B 6
Station Rd. LE7—6A 28
(Syston)
Station Rd. LE7—4H 11
(Thurnby)
Station Rd. LE8—2G 25
(Countesthorpe)
Station Rd. LE8—2H 21
(Wigston)
Station Rd. LE9—5A 24
(Croft)
Station Rd. LE9—4C 6
(Kirby Muxloe)
Station Rd. LE9—5G 19
(Narborough)
Station St. LE1—4G 9
Station St. LE8—4A 20
(Whetstone)
Station St. LE8—2G 21
(Wigston)
Station St. LE11—2E 27
Staveley Rd. LE5—6B 10
Steadman Av. LE9—3B 24
Stebbings Rd. LE2—6E 15
Steele Clo. LE5—4D 10
Steeple Clo. LE8—6C 16
Steeple Row. LE11—2F 27
Steins La. LE5—1E 11
Stenson Rd. LE3—1B 8
Stephenson Clo. LE6—2B 2
Stephenson Dri. LE3—2C 8
Stephenson Way. LE6—2A 2
Stewart Av. LE9—3F 19
Stewart Dri. LE11—1B 26
Steyning Cres. LE3—1H 7
Stiles, The. LE7—5B 28
Stirling Av. LE11—2C 26
Stirling St. LE5—3D 10
Stockland Rd. LE2—6E 15
Stocks Rd. LE7—2H 11
Stockton Rd. LE4—1B 10
Stockwell Rd. LE2—4A 16
Stokesby Rise. LE2—3D 20
Stokes Dri. LE3—1C 8
Stonebow Wlk. LE11—1A 26
Stonebridge St. LE5—3B 10
Stonechat Wlk. LE5—3A 10
Stonecroft. LE8—2F 25
Stonehaven Rd. LE4—4F 5
Stonehill Av. LE4—1D 4
Stonehurst Rd. LE3—2A 14
Stoneleigh Way. LE3—1D 8
Stonesby Av. LE2—6F 15
Stoneygate Av. LE2—2A 16
Stoneygate Ct. LE2—1A 16
Stoneygate Rd. LE2—1A 16
Stoneywell Rd. LE4—3F 3
Storer Rd. LE11—2E 27
Storey St. LE3—2E 9
Stornaway Rd. LE5—3G 11
Stoughton Av. LE2—2B 16
Stoughton Clo. LE2—4E 17
Stoughton Dri. LE5—1C 16
Stoughton Dri. N. LE5—6B 10
Stoughton Dri. S. LE2—2C 16
Stoughton La. LE2—1E 17
Stoughton Rd. LE2—2B 16
(Knighton)
Stoughton Rd. LE2—4D 16 to 2F 17
(Oadby)
Stoughton Rd. LE7—6H 11
Stoughton St. LE2—4H 9
Stoughton St. S. LE2—5H 9
Stour Clo. LE2—5G 17
Strasbourg Dri. LE4—5G 3
Stratford Rd. LE3—2B 14
Strathaven Rd. LE4—4E 5
Strathmore Av. LE4—5F 5
Strawberry Gdns. LE9—1E 19
Strensall Rd. LE2—1E 21
Stretton Rd. LE3—4D 8
Strollers Way. LE7—2D 28
Stroma Way. LE8—2H 25
Stroud Rd. LE5—3B 10
Stuart Rd. LE2—2D 20
Stuart St. LE3—6D 8
Stubbs Rd. LE4—2H 9
Sturdee Clo. LE2—1E 21
Sturdee Grn. LE2—6D 14
Sturdee Rd. LE2—6D 14
Styon Rd. LE3—1A 8
Sudeley Av. LE4—6B 4
Suffolk Clo. LE8—1G 21
Suffolk St. LE5—4C 10
Sulgrave Rd. LE5—2B 10
Sullivan Way. LE11—1E 27
Summer Lea Rd. LE5—4F 11
Sunbury Grn. LE5—2H 11
Sunningdale Rd. LE3—5F 7
Sunnycroft Rd. LE3—4C 8
Sunnyfield Clo. LE5—5F 11
Sunnyhill Rd. LE11—6E 27
Sun Way. LE3—6H 7
Surrey St. LE4—1H 9
Susan Av. LE5—6E 11
Sussex Rd. LE8—1F 21
Sussex St. LE5—3H 9
Sutherland St. LE2—5A 10
Sutton Av. LE4—6E 5
Sutton Clo. LE2—1E 23
Sutton Pl. LE4—6E 5
Sutton Rd. LE2—3G 15
Swainson Rd. LE4—1B 10
Swain St. LE2—4H 9
Swale Clo. LE2—4G 17
Swallow's Dale. LE7—1D 28
Swannington Rd. LE3—2D 8
Swanscombe Rd. LE2—2E 15
Swan St. LE3—3E 9
Swan St. LE11—2F 27
Sweetbriar Rd. LE3—6D 8
Swinford Av. LE2—2D 20
Swinford Ct. LE2—2E 21
Swingbridge Rd. LE11—1E 27
Swinstead Rd. LE5—6G 11
Swithland Av. LE4—1F 9
Swithland Clo. LE11—2B 26
Sybil Rd. LE3—2C 14
Sycamore Clo. LE2—2C 16
Sycamore Clo. LE7—6A 28
Sycamore Rd. LE4—1C 4
Sycamore St. LE8—4C 20
Sycamore Way. LE9—5G 19
Sykefield Av. LE3—5D 8
Sylvan Av. LE5—3A 10
Sylvan St. LE3—3D 8
Sylvan Way. LE3—5G 7
Syston By-Pass. LE7—2A 28
Syston Rd. LE7—3D 28
Syston St. E. LE1—2H 9
Syston St. W. LE1—2G 9
Sywell Dri. LE8—2C 22

Tadcaster Av. LE2—1E 21
Tadcaster Grn. LE2—1E 21
Tailby Av. LE5—2C 10
Tailor's Link. LE7—2C 28
Talbot La. LE1—4E 9
Talbot St. LE4—5C 4
Tamar Rd. LE2—5G 17
Tamar Rd. LE4—6G 5
Tamerton Rd. LE2—6E 15
Tansley Av. LE8—3G 21
Tarbat Rd. LE5—3G 11
Tatlow Rd. LE3—3G 7
Tatmarsh. LE11—2F 27
Taunton Clo. LE8—3A 22
Taunton Rd. LE3—5C 8
Taurus Clo. LE2—4H 9
Tavistock Dri. LE5—6C 10
Taylor Rd. LE1—2H 9
Tedworth Grn. LE4—3A 4
(in two parts)
Teesdale Clo. LE2—6F 9
Teignmouth Clo. LE5—6C 10
Teignmouth Wlk. LE5—6C 10
Telford Hall. LE11—4C 26
Telford Way. LE5—4H 11
Tempest Rd. LE4—3C 4
Temple Rd. LE5—4C 10
Tendring Dri. LE8—2D 22
Tennis Ct. Dri. LE5—2D 10
Tennyson Rd. LE11—2C 26
Tennyson St. LE2—6A 10
Tennyson St. LE9—3F 19
Tentercroft Av. LE7—4B 28
Terrace Cotts. LE9—5A 24
Tetuan Rd. LE3—3C 8
Tewkesbury St. LE3—4D 8
Thackeray St. LE2—2F 15
Thames St. LE1—2G 9
Thatcher Clo. LE4—4G 3
Thatcher's Corner. LE7—2D 28
Thirlmere Dri. LE11—6C 26
Thirlmere Rd. LE8—1C 22
Thirlmere St. LE2—6F 9
Thomasson Rd. LE5—4E 11
Thomas St. LE11—3H 27
Thomson Clo. LE4—3F 5
Thoresby St. LE5—3C 10
Thornby Gdns. LE8—2B 22
Thorndale Rd. LE4—2G 5
Thorney Clo. LE11—1C 26
Thornholme Clo. LE4—4H 3
Thornton Dri. LE9—4G 19
Thornville Clo. LE4—1B 10
Thorpe Acre Rd. LE11—2C 26
Thorpe Dri. LE8—6B 16
Thorpe Field Dri. LE4—1H 5
Thorpe Hill. LE11—3C 26
Thorpe St. LE3—4E 9
Thorpewell. LE5—4D 10
Thresher's Wlk. LE7—2D 28
Thurcaston Rd. LE4—1A to 5C 4
Thurcroft Clo. LE2—2D 20
Thurlaston La. LE9—1C 18
(Enderby)
Thurlaston La. LE9—5A 18
(Huncote)
Thurlby Rd. LE5—3B 10
Thurlington Rd. LE3—6B 8
Thurlow Rd. LE2—2G 15
Thurmaston Boulevd. LE4
(in three Parts) 4G 5
Thurmaston La. LE4 & LE5 —5H 5 to 1D 10
Thurnby Hill. LE7—4G 11
Thurnby La. LE2—2G 17
Thurncourt Clo. LE5—2F 11
Thurncourt Gdns. LE5—3H 11
Thurncourt Rd. LE5—2F to 3H 11
Thurnview Rd. LE5—6F 11
Tichborne St. LE2—5H 9
Tilford Cres. LE2—2E 21
Tilling Rd. LE4—4H 3
Tilling Wlk. LE4—4H 3
Tilton Dri. LE2—1D 22
Timber St. LE8—3F 21
Tinkers Dell. LE7—1C 28
Tithe St. LE5—3C 10
Tiverton Av. LE4—6E 5
Tiverton Clo. LE2—6F 17
Tiverton Rd. LE11—6E 27
Tolcarne Rd. LE5—1F 11
Tolchard Clo. LE5—4D 10
Tollemache Av. LE4—6B 4
Toller Rd. LE2—2A 16
Tollwell Rd. LE4—2H 3
Tolton Rd. LE4—4A 4
Tomlin Rd. LE4—1C 10
Toothill Rd. LE11—2F 27
Topcliffe Wlk. LE4—5A 4
Tophall Dri. LE8—2H 25
Torcross Clo. LE3—1H 7
Toronto Clo. LE1—3H 9
Torridon Clo. LE4—5H 3
Torrington Clo. LE8—4B 22
Torver Ho. LE2—1D 20
Totland Rd. LE3—2D 8
Tournament Rd. LE3—3G 7
Tovey Cres. LE2—6E 15
Towers Clo. LE9—6D 6
Towers Dri. LE9—5D 6
Tower St. LE1—5G 9
Towle Rd. LE3—1A 8
Town End Clo. LE2—3A 16
Town Hall Pas. LE11—3F 27
Townsend Clo. LE4—3F 5
Townsend Rd. LE9—1F 19
Trafford Rd. LE5—2C 10
Tranter Pl. LE4—6E 5
Treasure Clo. LE3—2G 7
Treaty Rd. LE3—3H 7
Tredington Rd. LE3—6D 2
Trelissick Clo. LE11—2B 26
Tremaine Dri. LE8—3A 22
Trenant Rd. LE2—6F 15
Trent Clo. LE2—5F 17
Trescoe Rise. LE3—4A 8
Trevino Dri. LE4—3F 5
Trevose Gdns. LE5—3G 11
Trinity Clo. LE7—6B 28
Trinity La. LE1—5G 9
Trinity Rd. LE8—4B 20
Trinity Rd. LE9—2H 19
Trinity St. LE11—3G 27
Triumph Rd. LE3—2G 7
Troon Way. LE4—3E to 4G 5
True Lovers Wlk. LE11—3E 27
Trueway Rd. LE5—1B 16
Truro Dri. LE8—3A 22
Tuckers Clo. LE11—4H 27
Tuckers Rd. LE11—4H 27
Tudor Clo. LE3—4E 9
Tudor Dri. LE2—5E 17
Tudor Dri. LE9—4B 24
Tudor Rd. LE3—3D 8
Tudor Wlk. LE3—4E 9
Tunstall Cres. LE4—1B 10
Turnbull Dri. LE3—3A 14
Turnbury Way. LE5—1C 16
Turner Av. LE11—4F 27
Turner Rise. LE2—6E 17
Turner Rd. LE5—2D 10
Turner St. LE1—5G 9
Turner Wlk. LE5—4D 10
Turnstone Wlk. LE5—3A 10
Turn St. LE7—5A 28
Turville Rd. LE3—6C 8
Tuskar Rd. LE5—2G 11
Tuxford Rd. LE4—4H 5
Twickenham Rd. LE2—2D 20
Twitten, The. LE2—3D 20

Twycross St. LE2—5A 10
Tyes End. LE4—5F 3
Tyler Av. LE11—1E 27
Tyler Rd. LE6—2C 6
Tyndale St. LE3—5D 8
Tynedale Clo. LE2—6G 17
Tynedale Rd. LE11—6B 26
Tyringham Rd. LE8—2C 22
Tyrell St. LE3—3D 8
Tysoe Hill. LE3—1H 7
Tythorn Dri. LE8—6H 15

Uldale Ho. LE2—1D 20
Ullswater Dri. LE2—6F 17
Ullswater St. LE2—5F 9
Ullswater Wlk LE2—6F 17
Ulverscroft Rd. LE4 & LE5
—2H 9
Ulverscroft Rd. LE11—6D 26
Una Av. LE3—3B 14
Unicorn St. LE4—1F 5
Union St. LE1—4F 9
Unity Rd. LE2—2G 7
University Clo. LE7—5B 28
University Rd. LE1—1G 15
University Rd. LE11—4B 26
Uplands Rd. LE2—5F 15
(Aylestone)
Uplands Rd. LE2—5E 17
(Oadby)
Up. Brown St. LE1—5F 9
Up. Charnwood St. LE2—3H 9
Up. Church St. LE7—4A 28
Up. George St. LE3—3G 9
Up. Hall Clo. LE5—2F 11
Up. Hall Grn. LE5—1F 11
Up. King St. LE1—5G 9
Up. Nelson St. LE1—5G 9
Up. New Wlk. LE1—5G 9
Up. Temple Wlk. LE4—5G 3
Up. Tichborne St. LE2—5H 9
Upperton Rise. LE3—5D 8
Upperton Rd. LE3—5D 8
Uppingham Clo. LE5—4F 11
Uppingham Rd. LE5 & LE7
—2B 10 to 4H 11
Upton Dri. LE8—2C 22
Uttoxeter Clo. LE4—5F 3
Uxbridge Rd. LE4—4E 5

Vale Clo. LE5—3F 11
Vale Clo. LE5—3F 11
Valence Rd. LE3—6C 8
Valentine Dri. LE2—5C 16
Valentine Rd. LE5—4G 11
Valiant Clo. LE3—2H 7
Valjean Cres. LE3—6D 6
Valley Dri. LE3—1G & 1H 13
Valley Rd. LE11—6D 26
Vancouver Rd. LE1—2G 9
Vandyke Clo. LE2—1E 23
Vann Wlk. LE4—6C 4
Vaughan Rd. LE2—4F 15
Vaughan St. LE3—3D 8
Vaughan Way. LE1—3F 9
Ventnor Rd. LE2—4B 16
Ventnor St. LE5—4B 10
Verdale Av. LE4—3H 5
Vernon Rd. LE2—4F 15
Vernon St. LE3—3E 9
Vestry St. LE1—4F 9
Vicarage Clo. LE9—3D 6
Vicarage La. LE5—5C 4
Vicarage La. LE5—2E 11
Victoria Av. LE2—5H 9
Victoria Ct. LE2—4D 16
Victoria Pas. LE1—5H 9
Victoria Rd. LE8—2G 15
Victoria Rd. E. LE5—1C 10
Victoria Rd. N. LE4—5D 4
Victoria St. LE1—1F 5
Victoria St. LE2—5A 28

Victoria St. LE8—1B 22
Victoria St. LE9—4G 19
Victoria St. LE11—3F 27
Victor Rd. LE3—1H 7
Victors Clo. LE2—6D 14
Viking Rd. LE8—1H 21
Villiers Hall. LE2—3D 16
Vincent Clo. LE3—3C 8
Vine St. LE1—3F 9
Vostock Clo. LE2—4H 9
Vulcan Rd. LE5—3A 10

Waddesdon Wlk. LE4—1B 10
Wade St. LE4—5B 4
Wain Dri. LE11—1B 26
Waingroves Wlk. LE4—4B4
Wakefield Pl. LE4—6E 5
Wakerley Rd. LE5—6C 10
Wakes Rd. LE8—1B 22
Walcote Rd. LE4—6G 5
Waldale Dri. LE2—1A 16
Waldron Dri. LE2—5F 17
Wale Rd. LE8—5B 20
Walker Rd. LE4—2C 4
(Birstall)
Walker Rd. LE4—3H 5
(Thurmaston)
Wallace Dri. LE6—1A 2
Wallace Rd. LE11—4E 27
Wallingford Rd. LE4—6B 4
Walnut Av. LE4—1C 4
Walnut Clo. LE2—6D 16
Walnut Gro. LE2—1C 20
Walnut Leys. LE9—3B 24
Walnut St. LE2—6F 9
Walnut St. LE2—6F 9
(Blaby)
Walnut Way. LE8—1G 25
(Countesthorpe)
Walpole Ct. LE3—5B 8
Walsgrave Av. LE5—5G 11
Walshe Rd. LE5—4E 11
Walsingham Cres. LE3—6F 7
Waltham Av. LE3—1B 14
Walton Clo. LE9—5E 7
Walton St. LE3—6D 8
Wand St. LE4—1G 9
Wanlip Av. LE4—1D 4
Wanlip La. LE4—1D 4
Wanlip Rd. LE7—6A 28
Wanlip St. LE1—2G 9
Wansbeck Gdns. LE5—2F 11
Wanstead Rd. LE4—4B 4
Ward Clo. LE2—4D 14
Wardens Wlk. LE3—6F 7
Wards End. LE11—3F 27
Wareham Rd. LE4—6C 20
War Memorial App. LE1
—6H 9
Warmsley Av. LE8—1A 22
Warner Pl. LE11—3G 27
Warner's La. LE11—2F 27
Warren Clo. LE5—1E 11
Warren Rd. LE3—3H 19
Warren St. LE3—3E 9
Warrington St. LE1—5H 9
Warwick Rd. LE8—1H 21
Warwick Rd. LE9 & LE8—5G 19
Warwick St. LE3—4D 8
Warwick Way. LE11—1C 26
Watchcrete Av. LE7—3D 28
Waterfield Clo. LE5—5E 11
Watergate. LE7—2D 28
Watergate La. LE3—4A 14
Waterloo Cres. LE8—2G 25
(Countesthorpe)
Waterloo Cres. LE8—1B 22
(Wigston)
Waterloo Way. LE1—6G 9
Watermead Way. LE4—4C 4
Waterside Clo. LE11—1G 27
Watling St. LE1—2F 9

Watson Rd. LE4—6E 5
Watts Clo. LE4—5F 3
Waveney Rise. LE2—5G 17
Waverley Rd. LE8—6D 20
(Blaby)
Waverley Rd. LE8—2F 21
(Wigston)
Waverley St. LE5—3D 10
Wavertree. LE2—3A 16
Wavertree Clo. LE8—2B 24
Wavertree Dri. LE4—4D 4
Wayfarer Clo. LE7—1D 28
Wayne Way, The. LE4—1C 4
Wayne Way, The. LE5—4C &
3C 10
Wayside Dri. LE2—5F 17
Wayside Rd. LE4—2F 5
Weaver Rd. LE5—2G 11
Weaver's Wynd. LE7—2C 28
Webb Clo. LE3—1F 13
Webster Rd. LE3—5A 8
Welbeck Av. LE4—6B 4
Welbeck Clo. LE8—6D 20
Welcombe Av. LE3—2A 14
Welcome Stranger Caravan Pk.
LE7—4B 28
Weldon Rd. LE8—1B 22
Welford Pl. LE1—4F 9
Welford Rd. LE2—5F 9 to 5A 16
Welford Rd. LE8—4C 20
(Blaby)
Welford Rd. LE8—3B 22
(Wigston)
Welham Wlk. LE4—4H 5
Welland St. LE2—5H 9
Welland Vale Rd. LE5—5F 11
Wellesbourne Dri. LE3—6D 2
Welles St. LE1—4E 9
Wellgate Av. LE4—1C 4
Wellhouse Clo. LE8—4A 22
Wellinger Way. LE3—5A 8
Wellington St. LE1—5G 9
Wellington St. LE7—5A 28
Wellington St. LE11—3G 27
Wembley Rd. LE3—4F 7
Wembury Gdns. LE4—4A 4
Wendy's Clo. LE5—3G 11
Wenlock Way. LE4—5H 5
Wensleydale Rd. LE8—3C 22
Wensley Rise. LE2—2D 20
Wentbridge Rd. LE4—5F 5
Went Rd. LE4—2C 4
Wentworth Rd. LE3—4D 8
Wesley Clo. LE6—2B 6
Wesley St. LE4—5C 4
Wessex Dri. LE3—4H 7
West Av. LE2—1H 15
West Av. LE8—1H 21
W. Bond St. LE3—3F 9
Westbourne St. LE4—1G 9
W. Bridge St. LE1—4E 9
Westbury Rd. LE2—2G 15
Westcotes Dri. LE3—5D 8
Westdale Av. LE2—2B 20
Westdown Dri. LE4—3G 5
West Dri. LE5—2D 10
Westerby Clo. LE8—6B 16
Westerdale Rd. LE8—2D 22
Western Boulevd. LE2—5E 9
Western Dri. LE8—5C 20
Westernhay Rd. LE2—2A 16
Western Pk. Boulevd. LE3
—4H 7

Westhill Rd. LE3—4B 8
W. Holme St. LE3—5E 9
Westleigh Av. LE3—6D 8
Westleigh Rd. LE3—6D 8
Westleigh Rd. LE2—3E 21
Westleigh Rd. LE3—6D 8
Westmeath Av. LE5—4E 11
Westminster Rd. LE2—2B 16
Westmorland Av. LE4—6E 5
Westmorland Av. LE8—2G 21
Westmorland Av. LE11—5C 26
Westover Rd. LE3—1H 13
West St. LE1—5G 9
West St. LE3—6C 2
West St. LE7—5A 28
West St. LE8—3C 20
West St. LE9—2F 19
West St. Open. LE3—5E 9
Westview Av. LE2—4F 5
West Wlk. LE1—5G 9
Wetherby Rd. LE4—4F 5
Wexford Clo. LE2—6G 17
Weymouth Clo. LE8—4D 22
Weymouth St. LE4—1H 9
Whaddon Dri. LE11—5G 27
Wharf St. LE4—1F 5
Wharf St. N. LE1—3G 9
Wharf St. S. LE1—3G 9
Wharf Way. LE2—2C 20
Wharncliffe Rd. LE11—3G 27
Wheatland Clo. LE2—6G 17
Wheatland Dri. LE11—5G 27
Wheatland Rd. LE4—3A 4
Wheatlands Dri. LE8—2G 25
Wheatley Rd. LE4—4H 3
Wheatleys Rd. LE4—2F 5
Wheat St. LE1—3G 9
Wheeldale. LE8—2C 22
Wheeldale Clo. LE4—5A 4
Wheldon Rd. LE11—1D 26
Whetstone Gorse La. LE8
—1C 24
Whiles La. LE4—2D 4
Whinchat Rd. LE4—1B 4
Whiston Clo. LE5—3F 11
White Barn Dri. LE9—3A 24
Whitefield Rd. LE4—5C 4
White Ga. LE11—2G 27
Whitehall Rd. LE5—5E 11
Whitehead Cres. LE8—1A 22
White Horse La. LE4—1G 9
Whitehouse Av. LE11—4G 27
White Ho. Clo. LE8—3F 23
Whiteoaks Rd. LE2—1F 23
Whitesand Clo. LE3—1C 8
Whitley Clo. LE3—1C 8
Whitman Clo. LE3—4H 7
Whitteney Dri. LE2—6D 14
Whittier Rd. LE2—3G 15
Whittington Dri. LE6—1B 6
Whitwell Row. LE4—5H 9
Whitwick Way. LE3—1D 8
Wicken Rise. LE8—1B 22
Wickham Rd. LE2—6E 17
Wicklow Dri. LE5—3D 10
Wigley Rd. LE5—1F 11
Wigston Clo. LE2—5D 14
Wigston Rd. LE2—6C 16
Wigston Rd. LE8—4C 20
Wigston St. LE1—4G 9
Wigston St. LE8—2H 25
Wilberforce Rd. LE3—6D 8
Wild Rose Wlk. LE7—1D 28
William Pk. Rd. LE9—5F 19
William Rowlett Hall. LE2
—5E 9
Wiliams Clo. LE9—5G 19
William St. LE1—3H 9
William St. LE11—3E 27
Willoughby Rd. LE8—2F to
6F 25
Willow Brook Rd. LE5—2A 10
Willow Clo. LE9—6G 19
Willow Dri. LE8—1H 25

Willow Pk. Dri. LE8—1A 22
Willow Rd. LE8—5C 20
Willow Rd. LE11—6E 27
Willow St. LE1—2G 9
Wilmington Ct. LE11—4H 27
Wilmore Cres. LE3—6H 7
Wilne St. LE2—5A 10
Wilnicott Rd. LE3—2A 14
Wilsford Clo. LE8—4A 22
Wilshere Clo. LE9—5C 6
Wilson Rd. LE8—3F 21
Wilson St. LE2—4A 10
Wilstone Clo. LE11—4B 26
Wilton Av. LE11—5G 27
Wilton Clo. LE2—6F 17
Wilton St. LE1—3G 9
Wiltshire Rd. LE4—6A 4
Wiltshire Rd. LE1—1H 21
Wimbledon St. LE1—4G 9
Wimborne Clo. LE8—3A 22
Wimbourne Rd. LE2—4B 16
Winchendon Clo. LE5—2B 10
Winchester Av. LE3—6G 8
Winchester Av. LE8—3C 20
Winchester Clo. LE8—5D 20 to
2F 25
Windermere Av. LE8—6B 24
Windermere Rd. LE8—1C 22
Windermere St. LE2—6F 9
Winders Way. LE2—5E 15
Windley Rd. LE2—5G 15
Windmill Av. LE4—1D 4
Windmill Rise. LE8—2B 2
Windmill Rd. LE11—3H 27
Windrush Dri. LE2—4G 17
Windsor Av. LE2—3F 21
Windsor Av. LE4—6D 4
Windsor Clo. LE2—7F 23
Windsor Rd. LE11—1C 26
Winforde Cres. LE3—5H 7
Wingfield St. LE4—6D 4
Winifred St. LE2—5F 9
Winslow Dri. LE8—1B 22
Winslow Grn. LE5—1F 11
Winstanley Dri. LE3—5B 8
Winster Dri. LE4—1G 5
Winston Av. LE4—1G 5
Winterburn Way. LE11—4B 26
Wintersdale Rd. LE5—4F 11
Winterton Clo. LE4—1H 5
Winton Av. LE3—1D 14
Wistow Rd. LE8—6G 23
(Newton Harcourt)
Wistow Rd. LE8—3B 22
(Wigston)
Withcote Av. LE5—4F 11
Withens Clo. LE3—3B 8
Witherdell. LE4—5F 3
Woburn Clo. LE2—1D 20
Woburn Clo. LE8—2C 22
Woburn Clo. LE11—2B 26
Wodboy St. LE1—2G 9
Wokingham Av. LE2—2E 21
Wolds, The. LE7—1D 28
Wollaton Av. LE11—2C 26
Wolsey St. LE1—1E 9
Wolsey Way. LE7—6A 28
Wolverton Rd. LE3—1D 14
Woodbank. LE2—2C 20
Woodbank Rd. LE2—5A 16
Woodbank Rd. LE6—3A 2
Woodbridge Rd. LE2—5H 9
Woodbrook Rd. LE11—5D 26
Woodcote Rd. LE3—3A 14
Woodcroft Av. LE2—4G 15
Wood End. LE3—3B 8
Woodfield Rd. LE2—4E 17
Woodford Clo. LE8—4A 22
Woodgate. LE3—3D 8
Wood Ga. LE11—3F 27
Woodgate Dri. LE4—1B 4

Woodgate Dri. LE11—4E 27
Woodgon Rd. LE7—2D 2
Woodgreen Rd. LE4—6F 5
Woodgreen Wlk. LE4—1B 10
Woodhall Clo. LE3—4H 7
Wood Hill. LE5—3A 10
Woodland Av. LE2—2A 16
Woodland Av. LE9—3F 19
Woodland Dri. LE3—1H 13
Woodland Rd. LE5—3B 10
Woodlands Dri. LE6—2A 2
Woodlands Dri. LE11—5E 27
Woodlands La. LE9—3D 6
Woodlands, The. LE8—2G 25
(Countesthorpe)
Woodlands, The. LE—1C 22
(Wigston)
Woodley Rd. LE6—1B 6
Woodman's Chase. LE7—2C 28
Woodnewton Dri. LE5—5F 11
Woods Clo. LE2—4F 17
Woodshawe Rise. LE3—1A 14
Woodside Clo. LE4—1B 10
Woodside Rd. LE2—1G 23
Woodstock Clo. LE4—4A 4
Woodstock Rd. LE4—4A 4
Wood St. LE1—3G 9
Woodthorpe Av. LE11—5G 27
Woodthorpe Rd. LE11—5G 27
Woodville Gdns. LE8—6A 16
Woodville Rd. LE3—4C 8
Woolsthorpe Wlk. LE8—2B 10
Wootton Rise. LE2—6E 15
Worcester Av. LE1—1E 5
Worcester Dri. LE8—2G 21
Worcester Rd. LE2—4E 15
Wordsworth Cres. LE9—3E 19
Wordsworth Rd. LE2—2G 15
Wordsworth Rd. LE11—2C 26
Worrall Clo. LE5—5H 7
Worrall Rd. LE3—5H 7
Worthington St. LE2—5A 10
Wreford Cres. LE5—3H 11
Wren Clo. LE2—3F 15
Wroxall Way. LE3—1D 8
Wyatt Clo. LE5—3G 7
Wycliffe St. LE1—4F 9
Wycombe Rd. LE5—2C 10
Wykeham Clo. LE5—5H 7
Wylam Clo. LE3—1C 8
Wymar Clo. LE4—5H 3
Wyndale Dri. LE4—4B 28
Wyndale Rd. LE2—4H 15
Wyndham Clo. LE2—4F 17
Wynfield Rd. LE3—4C 8
Wyngate Dri. LE3—5C 8
Wynthorpe Rise. LE3—5B 8
Wynton Clo. LE8—5D 20
Wythburn Clo. LE11—6C 26
Wyvern Av. LE4—5F 5
Wyville Row. LE3—2B 14

Yardley Dri. LE3—5H 15
Yarmouth St. LE1—2G 9
Yarwell Dri. LE8—2C 22
Yelverton Av. LE5—6F 11
Yeoman La. LE1—4G 9
Yeoman's Dale. LE7—1D 28
Yeoman St. LE1—4G 9
Yews Rd., The. LE2—4E 17
Yews. The. LE2—4E 17
Yew Tree Dri. LE3—3G 7
York Rd. LE1—5F 9
York Rd. LE11—3E 27
Yorkshire Rd. LE4—6E 5
York St. LE1—4G 9
Yukon Way. LE1—3G 9

Zetland Wlk. LE4—3A 4

Every possible care has been taken to ensure that the information shown in this publication is accurate, and whilst the Publishers would be grateful to learn of any errors, they regret they can accept no responsibility for any expense or loss thereby caused.

Printed and bound in Great Britain by Halstan & Co. Ltd., Plantation Road, Amersham, Bucks.